Nathan's Footprints

Seven Decades of Personal Anecdotes
(From the 1940s into the 21st Century)

By
Dr. Nathan J. Johnson

PublishAmerica
Baltimore

First printing

ISBN: 1-4137-3394-8
PUBLISHED BY PUBLISHAMERICA, LLLP
www.publishamerica.com
Baltimore

Printed in the United States of America

Nathan's Footprints

Seven Decades of Personal Anecdotes (From the 1940s into the 21st Century)

This book is dedicated to my wife Charlotte for her willingness to proofread my work, her timely advice, and her frequent words of inspiration.

Foreword

A few years ago I received a "book-to-be-completed" blank copy from my son Eric and his wife Denise. As I looked through the pages at the questions and the sparse space for responses to the questions, I was reminded of a newspaper reporter's question to me as a new small college president.

The reporter was interviewing me for an article in a local newspaper and wanted to know, among other things, my philosophy of education. I looked him in the eyes and told him that if he wanted to spend a week with me, I could share with him some of my philosophy of education. By spending time with me, I could share with him part of my philosophy of education regarding curriculum, staff development, hiring licensed and non-licensed employees, evaluation and termination of employees, budgeting, state college boards, state and federal departments of education laws, community involvement, data privacy, security, discipline, long-range planning, administration vs. leadership skills, and the like.

A philosophy of education has always been a work-in-progress for me and was certainly beyond the scope of the reporter's hour-long interview. He called me a "thinker" in the article that he wrote, although I'm not certain why.

So it was with the "book-to-be-completed." There just wasn't adequate space provided for the responses to the questions. I must admit, however, that the book did get me thinking about writing some of my life experiences, rather than my philosophy-of-life, etcetera. And, so I began writing and one anecdote led to another and so evolved, *Nathan's Footprints*, spanning seven decades.

I hope that you will enjoy these highly reliable anecdotes from my life. Happy trails to you.

The Nineteen Forties

The Fire in the Woods

My brother David, who was nearly thirteen at the time and closest in age to me, had a paper route. He was nearly three-years older than I, and the money he made from the paper route enabled him to have more money than any boy that I knew in the neighborhood. Sometimes, David bought us all candy and took us to the movies with his paper route wealth. The price of a movie for kids under fifteen was twelve cents; and for another ten cents, you could buy a cup of soda pop and a small bag of popcorn.

David was a great big-brother — shared a lot, and included me a lot in his adventures. One day in the middle of July, David had this grand idea. He wrote a note that would enable him to buy cigarettes at Richard's Market Basket, a friendly neighborhood grocery store about two blocks from where we lived, on the west side of Austin, Minnesota. He signed my mother's name and bought a pack of Lucky Strike cigarettes, some candy, and four bottles of Orange Crush soda pop. I was always intrigued by the Orange Crush soda being distributed in dark brown bottles. Then David, two neighbor brothers named Smiley and George, and I headed off across the open fields to the Second Woods, a trek of about a mile.

We were having a good time walking, drinking Orange Crush, stopping to pee, and laughing and swearing as little boys often do when they are away from adults. After awhile, we had arrived at the Seconds Woods. David and Smiley were our older brothers; and therefore, the only ones allowed to smoke. One of David's friends, his real name was William, but his nickname was "Smiley," did everything that David told him to do, it seemed to me. William, from my perspective, was not a "Bill" and never seemed like a "Smiley" to me. Smiley was a couple of years older than I, didn't smile very much, and had a goofy horse-laugh; I don't know how else to describe it. Smiley's brother George and I were about the same age and went to the same elementary school.

My brother David said that George (sometimes I called him "Georgee-Porgy") and I were too young to smoke and that smoking would stunt our growth. I was pretty short already so that seemed okay to me (some adults called me a toe-headed-runt, which defined at the time meant I was a bleach-blonde little twerp). Anyway, I didn't know how to smoke. The way David and Smiley coughed and gagged when they smoked didn't look like much fun to me anyway.

Georgee-Porgy told me that smoking was like eating horse turds. I thought that was pretty funny, but I knew Georgee-Porgy had never smoked 'cause he was too big of a chicken to do that. I considered, in my minds-eye, him eating horse turds and the thought was amusing; but I knew it was just talk from Georgee-Porgy. I was positive that Georgee-Porgy had never smoked or, for that matter, ever tasted horse turds. Georgee-Porgy liked to talk, that much I knew.

David and Smiley decided that we needed to build a little fire. I guessed that somehow building a fire in the middle of July would fit into the big-boys' idea of the ideal smoking environment. So we all rummaged around the woods and gathered up small pieces of dry wood and piled it in a circle. The big-boys were smoking and the small-boys were eating candy. We were having fun. Georgee-Porgy and I climbed up a small tree to watch as David used candy wrappers and matches to start a fire with the dry wood.

After the fire started burning, David and Smiley decided that they would do some "Indian-dancing" around the fire. I guess they had seen some dancing like that done in some movie or read about it in school. Maybe my brother and his friend dancing around the fire was a sort of spontaneous combustion of "boys-around-fire." They took off their shirts and were dancing around the fire and whooping and yelling like wild animals. From our elevated tree vantage point, George and I thought it was a pretty funny scene.

We were really having a great time and I thought, *Some day I will smoke and dance around a fire, too*. Then there was a great gust of wind and the small fire started to spread in the July dry grass. First, David and Smiley tried to beat out the spreading flames with some sticks, but that didn't work at all. Then David picked up his shirt to beat the fire out, and he yelled at Smiley to do the same. They were trying to beat the fire out with their shirts, but the wind had picked up and they couldn't keep up with the fire. It was too dry and too windy and the fire was spreading. Soon they dropped their flaming shirts. In a matter of seconds, the fun had turned to terror. The fire had spread so rapidly. It was the first time that I had ever seen panic on my big-brother's face. David yelled at us to get out of the tree and run for our lives. In a matter of minutes, the fire had spread from our little smoking nest in the Second Woods, to the surrounding dry grass, and into the farmer's adjacent ripened field of oats.

Georgee-Porgy and I were out of the tree in a flash and ran at full speed towards home. We stopped when we were out of breath. We had run probably two hundred yards without looking back. We were huffing and puffing and waiting for our brothers. We could see the spreading flames and the smoke billowing into the sky. We were hot, out of breath, and most of all we were scared.

The big-boys were bare-chested after they had left their burning-shirts and came running when they figured the fire was out of control. George and I were both scared-to-death and Georgee-Porgy was crying when Smiley and David reached us. David and Smiley were hot and sweaty with blotches of ashes on their chests, arms, and faces; but most of all they looked really frightened.

We huddled very briefly in the ripened oat field, some distance from the blazing brush, trees, and oats. William said to his brother George, "Stop crying or I'll kick your ass!"

Then my brother David, who was a master at creating and selling ideas, concocted a story that we would need to swear a death-oath-to, or he said he would, "Pound us down so far into the ground that we'd be using our elbows for walking, and our ears for crutches."

Wow, I thought, *this must really be serious since my brother had never before talked of pounding me into the ground or beating me up.*

The gist of the concocted story was that the four of us had been sitting around in the Second Woods telling stories when some "big-boys" came by who taunted us and flipped their lighted cigarettes at us. We left when they told us, "Get the hell out of here or we will kick your asses."

What really concerned me at the time was that I would probably never be able to convincingly say the "ass-word" to any adult. I had rarely said ass to my friends, let alone an adult. I had mulled this over in my mind. *"Kicking our rumps," just didn't have a convincing ring to it.*

With that foolproof story in mind the four of us set off running for home to tell my mom to call the fire department. Our home, by the far southwestern edge of the now-burning oat field, was the first home we would come to. As small boys, we assumed that our home was out of danger from the fire in the Second Woods. One of my cousins later told me that she had seen the smoke from the fire seven miles away. The fire department could do little to stop that burning oat field once it had gotten out of control. The Austin Fire Department at that time had only one rural fire truck. Ironically, although we lived on the edge of town, the closest fire hydrant was located just across the street. When the fire had gotten close to the southern edge of the oat field, the firemen were able to put the fire out with the hoses connected to the fire hydrant on our street, as well as the hydrant located a block east of our street. The eastern edge of the Second Woods and the complete oat field burned to the ground that July day.

For historical purposes, the fire was started by some big boys throwing lighted cigarettes, and that's the truth.

The Ice Delivery Man

The several years that we lived in the house at 1209 West 7th Street, we had an ice box; and I can remember being intrigued by that whole process. The iceman would drive up in a big truck and water would be dripping out of the back of it. Of course, I would always announce to my mother that the iceman had arrived when the truck pulled into our gravel driveway.

The iceman wore a kind of canvas apron that split at his crotch and tied around his legs. It kind of reminded me of the chaps that I saw cowboys wear in the movies (by that time I had probably seen a total of three cowboy movies). I remember asking him why he wore that outfit, and he said that it helped to keep him dry. He wore a funny cloth hat that didn't have a visor on it and he wasn't a very friendly guy. I guess if you lugged ice around summer and winter all day long, it kind of cooled your personality.

I vividly recall that the muscles in the iceman's arms rippled when he grabbed some big metal tongs and clamped onto a chunk of ice for our little icebox. He would then carry the new block of ice into our enclosed front porch where the icebox was located. I always hung around when he came during the summer months for the little piece of ice that was nearly all melted in the fridge when it was replaced with the fresh ice. I would suck on that little piece of ice; and then when my mouth got too cold, I would rub it on my forehead to cool down. My mother always paid "mister cool" after the ice was installed; and sometimes after he had gone, she would wistfully say, "Some day we're going to have a refrigerator."

One of our neighbors at the time, the Bells, had a fridge; I had seen it when I had been over at their house to play with my friend David. I didn't understand how refrigerators worked, especially after David's

15

dad had given me a complicated mechanical explanation.

Mr. Bell, who sometimes wore his old WW II navy clothes, was always winking at me when he explained something. Maybe he thought I couldn't comprehend his narratives, and sometimes he was right. I guess he was a stockbroker or something. My dad always thought he was "a pain-in-the-ass," and I never really knew what that meant. Maybe it was because Mr. Bell had a brand new 1947 Plymouth. I don't know.

Mrs. Bell, who was always kind and friendly to me, also had a modern convenience for ironing clothes. It was called a mangle, which seemed to me like a strange name to describe something that was supposed to make some clothes look nice. To describe the machine and how it worked, or didn't work, should be written about by someone who cares about "mangles."

We didn't have any air conditioning in our home on 7th Street, not even a fan, like some of my friends had in their homes. Before we moved from that home, my dad had purchased us a fan and a new refrigerator from a store downtown. I had heard my dad discussing those purchases with my mother, and he had told her that we just had to put down about twenty-five percent of the purchase price, I think, and then make monthly payments until it was paid. I didn't understand those business deals, but my mom was sure happy with the fan and the new fridge. I didn't miss the iceman coming after that purchase at all, but my friend, Bill the milkman still made his deliveries.

Over the next ten years, Mom and Dad bought a lot of furniture on their good name from a store called Mier Wolf & Sons in Austin. According to Mom and Dad, they really got good deals at that furniture store; and they could pay for their purchases over a period of time. I didn't understand who owned the store because I had a friend at school named Mier Wolf and his dad's name was Bob. Sometimes when we were downtown, my mom would send me into that store to make a payment and my friend Mier's dad, Bob, was always very friendly to me.

Although my mom and dad bought a number of pieces of furniture and appliances over time when buying on credit was emerging in this country, they were always happy with the simple things in life. They never knew extravagance, nor did they ever try to portray that they had it. I can't remember once when either my mom or dad wished for something beyond their means, but that doesn't mean that they didn't do it.

Our Milk Man

My favorite deliveryman was a milkman named Bill. Bill came three days a week and each time delivered nine quarts of milk in glass bottles. With three older brothers and an older sister, we drank a lot of milk. My mother had a little dipper that she would insert in the top of the bottle and this helped her skim off the cream. She used that cream for baking and making whipped-cream for desserts.

Bill the milkman always wore a white shirt, white pants, and white hat with a black shiny visor. The hat looked kind of like one of those hats that you'd see policemen wearing, except this one was white.

Bill's name was printed just above the Marigold Dairy logo on his shirt, but I would never forget Bill's name. He was a friendly guy and always had something nice to say to me. Sometimes in the summer, he'd questioned me about where I had gotten my black hair. I always got a kick out of that 'cause my hair was as bleach-blond as could be, others called me a toe-head. I never quite understood that toe-head expression, but I figured it was some kind of reference to my sun-bleached hair. Bill the milkman was my friend and I remember his friendly smile to this day.

The Coal Man

I don't remember how frequently that we had coal delivered to our house; but if I was home from school, I was there to help him. He would back his truck up our graveled driveway until he was next to our house. Then he would swing a wooden chute that was attached to the side of the truck towards one of the basement windows. I would run down into the basement to direct the flow of coal into the proper location.

Prior to going downstairs, I would go out on the front porch where we had boxed old clothes to give to the needy. I would find an old jacket and cap of my dad's so I had on the proper attire to direct the coal operation. Sometimes, the sleeves of the jacket would drag along the floor and I would roll them up the best that I could. This was not a fashion statement, you understand, but a coal miner's wardrobe. There was work to be done.

Directing the coal into the proper location was not an easy job for an eight-year-old, as the dust would fill the air when the coal hit the floor. Sometimes, I would pick up a piece of the coal and rub it on my hands and face. Then, I would go upstairs and announce to my mother that Bart, the coal man, and I were done unloading the coal.

My mother would notice the coal on my hands and face and note that working with coal was a hard and dirty business, and she appreciated the work that I had done. She would give me a hug and a kiss and then she would direct me to get washed up. I would wash away most of the coal evidence of hard work. For the remainder of the day, I left some of the coal streaks as evidence to show my brothers, sister, and dad that I was a working contributor in our family. I was the son of a butcher, but I was a novice in the management of coal transportation and delivery.

The Mink Farm

About a quarter of a mile north of our home in the northwestern city limits of Austin, on the way to the big woods, was a mink farm owned by some of our neighbors. This was a place where a neighbor tried to eke out some part-time revenue by raising mink to sell to furriers. The mink were all in little boxed cages about two feet wide by four feet long and about two feet high. Each cage had a small wooden shelter at one end and the whole cage was surrounded by chicken wire. There were approximately twenty-five to thirty of those cages at the mink farm, as I recall. I remember that there was a distinct smell of unclean animals and feces. I could not determine which smell it was at that time. The whole animal confinement area was probably only a couple of acres.

We were told by the owners of the mink farm, in no uncertain terms, to stay away from that place because the mink were very nervous animals. We were also told that mink would get so excited when strangers were around that they would eat their young, which wasn't entirely true because I had sneaked up there unobserved and looked at those mink a few times. Those adult mink were nervous little critters, I'll grant you that; but I never once saw them eat a little one. There were no fences to keep out trespassers of that little mink enterprise.

On a couple of summer occasions in 1948, I remember creeping in the tall grass up close to that mink farm when the owners were going to shoot an old horse for mink feed. It was a kind of scary experience and yet exciting in a sad kind of way. One old man with baggy pants and a ragged straw-hat stood with about a four-foot-long rope tied to the halter of the horse, while another man, who always needed a shave, stood about twenty feet away and shot the horse in the head with a high-powered rifle. It only took one shot. Those old horses were sad-looking and sway-backed. Once the shot was fired, with the sound ricocheting off of the small shed, the man would let loose of the rope, and the horse would wobble and crumble to the ground like a ton-of-bricks. I figured that the rope-holder must have had a lot of trust in the shooter.

The whole process of shooting horses for mink feed was repulsive to me. I always felt sorry for the horse and the guy holding the rope. I had seen a number of old horses like that pulling a one-bottom plow on small farms, and their eyes always looked so sad. I was always angry at the shooter, because shooting a horse didn't seem very dignified to me. I couldn't imagine why those mink were so important that they had to shoot horses for them to eat. I didn't care much to watch them butcher up the fallen horses, because that was a pretty messy scene, so I would crawl off undetected, I thought, by the two men hard at their work.

After they butchered the horses, they hauled the meat to a small tin-shed, with a meat-grinder in it, where they ground up the horsemeat into feed for the mink. They didn't have any running water up at the mink farm, and I can remember Dale, one of the big teenage neighbor boys, lugging two five-gallon cans of water in each hand up there every day. Imagine that, two in each hand! That was nearly twenty gallons of water that he would carry. That big husky teenager would stop every once in awhile to rest when he was making those daily trips. One time when Dale stopped to rest, I tried to lift up just one of those buckets and I couldn't do it. I was eight years old.

One summer in the late forties, one of the neighbor boys, who was younger than I, was up at the mink farm snooping around, I guess. Somehow he got into that shed where they ground up the butchered horses into mink meat. And, somehow the grinder was started and somehow some of his shirt sleeve got caught up in the conveyor belt of the machinery, and somehow that efficient grinding machine pulled his hand into that horse-meat-for-mink-feed grinder. It all happened in a matter of seconds, and it must have been an excruciating painful experience for an innocent boy. A tragedy had occurred and little Steve, off on some sort of a covert mission, lost his hand and his left arm up to the elbow. He nearly died from loss of blood before he arrived at the hospital.

I don't know why that boy was up there messing around. I don't know how that boy was able to get into that shed. I don't know how that meat-grinding machine was started. I don't know why that grinding machine jammed, but if it had kept on grinding it surely would have cost that innocent boy his life. Furthermore, I don't know to this day who started up that meat grinder, or for that matter, who came to the boy's rescue and got him to the hospital. Nobody ever really felt it necessary to explain to an eight-year-old what happened that mid-summer day, but someone had surely started that meat grinder, and someone had surely helped him get free from the machine.

I heard my dad tell my mom that the switch for the meat grinder was some seven feet off the ground so nobody could figure out how little Steve had gotten the grinder started. The boy later said that some big kid had started the machine, but the identity of that mystery kid was never solved. The owners of that mink farm speculated that maybe the injured boy had flipped the machine switch on with a shovel handle or a stick. I had never been so curious that I had gone inside of that shed, but I admit I had once or twice peaked inside through the cracks in the door. The shed had such a foul odor, as I recall, and there were always a lot of flies buzzing around. When the men were working in the meat-grinding shed, the sound of that horse-meat-grinding machine was sufficient warning for me to stay away.

The parents of the injured boy sued the owners of the mink farm, who were George A. Hormel meat-packing friends of my dad's. I remember that my dad, a Hormel meat cutter, had to take off work and lost pay, so that he could testify as a character witness for the owners of the mink farm. My dad was as honest as they come, and I'm certain that his testimony was good for the owners of the mink farm.

Some kind of settlement was awarded to the boy who lost his hand and a good share of his arm, but I never knew how much. I thought it would never be enough to replace that hand and arm.

That mink farm was the closest that my mom ever came to having a mink coat. One time, a while after that boy's accident, when some adults were talking in our home, I heard one of them say that the only animal that ever really needed a mink coat was a mink. It made sense to me.

My dad put the fear of God into me about staying away from that mink farm after that boy's accident. Dad could really do that well and I never did go up there to that mink farm again. You can be certain of that, and that's the truth.

Hookin' Buses

Two of my older brothers, Raymond and David, taught me the skill of "hookin' buses," the winter that I was nine years old. After a really heavy snowstorm, we would walk down to the corner of 7th Street and Euclid and hide behind some big spruce trees. We would be all dressed up in our winter jackets, caps, mittens, and buckle-up overshoes. Approximately every thirty minutes, a city public transportation bus would stop at that corner to discharge or pick up passengers. Our best opportunity for hookin' buses was between five and six o'clock when it was dark and the last bus came by at 6 p.m. Friday nights the buses ran until 9 p.m. so we were always praying for snow on Fridays.

When the bus stopped, we would run out from behind the trees, squat down in a sitting position, and hold onto the rear bumper of the bus. The streets were rarely plowed in those days; and even if they had been sanded, it really didn't matter. I never held onto the bus for more than two blocks during my rookie season, and then the bus would stop at the next stop sign. Sometimes, Raymond and David would "hook-the-bus" downtown, a distance of about a mile and a half. The worst thing about the rear bumper bus ride was the smell of the diesel exhaust. I never fell off once on my short rides. Hookin' buses made the Minnesota winters a little shorter when I was nine years old and provided new experiences for a boy in 1949.

The Nineteen Fifties

The Black Patent-Leather Purse

We had moved from the very northwestern part of Austin in the summer of 1950 to the very northeast side of the city. We had moved from an old house to a one-year-old new house built by my Uncle Lawrence, my mother's brother. It was a fancy house, from my limited perspective, that included a built-in dishwasher in 1950, which my mother never got accustomed to and rarely used. She preferred to wash the dishes by hand. I would estimate that the new house probably cost in the neighborhood of 12,000 dollars, which was a lot of money at the time for our family. My family lived in that house until 1998, when my mother moved into an independent living federally-subsidized senior retirement center funded by Housing and Urban Development (HUD).

As the summer days passed in my new neighborhood, I got to know a couple of the neighbor boys better and better. Paul, the one who had brandished a rifle aiming it right at my head the first day I lived there, later told me that he had just been kidding. He said he didn't even have any bullets in the gun at the time. *Ha ha,* I remember thinking, *that was really funny, what a weirdo.* The other boy that lived right behind our house was Jimmy. He was a kind boy with freckles who seemed to be always looking for adventure. Jimmy was taller than me and kind of skinny, and Paul was bowlegged and about the same size as me.

Not too far from where we lived was a make-shift city dump, and we used to go there always hoping to find some new treasure. This was way before people in our part of the country went to garage sales looking for great buys and calling it "antiquing." The dump was, as you'd expect, filled with discarded junk, old tires, broken furniture, broken glass, and various other kinds of debris.

27

One day when my two buddies and I were out at the dump, Jimmy picked up an old shiny black purse and we took it home to his garage. Paul said it was expensive because it was made from patent leather. Later, I had Paul try to explain to me what patent leather was because it was a new term for me. The purse wasn't very big, maybe about eight inches high and twelve inches wide; and it didn't look like it was even damaged. We found, upon closer inspection, that it had a secret compartment inside that was covered by a piece of cloth material and zipped shut. We wondered why anyone would throw away a perfectly good purse like that, especially since it had a secret compartment. Jimmy said that since he had found it, it was his; and he might wrap it up and give it to his mother for Christmas.

We spent the next few days playing war games, since we had relatives who were veterans of World War II or would soon be fighting over in Korea. We were kids without television and life went on.

There was Delbert, a tall gangly kid a couple of blocks away. We were always trying to get him to make us some play army rifles. Delbert was a neat guy who seemed to have more teeth than his mouth could hold. He was always busy and never seemed to be able to play with us. He was always practicing on the piano or drawing pictures on an easel inside his house. Delbert had carved a replica of an army rifle for Paul, and Jimmy and I both wanted one just like it. Our mission was to just get him to forget that piano for awhile and get to the important things in life, like making us some army guns. We didn't succeed in getting ol' Delbert to carve us those much-needed weapons that summer.

There were two beer joints that had new black and white television sets in downtown Austin at that time. The reception was poor since they were picking up the television signals from two television stations located in Minneapolis and St. Paul, approximately one hundred miles away. My friends and I had biked downtown in the evenings a number of times and tried to get a peak through the window of the bar on Main Street that had a television set. There was a lot of snow on the television screen, and about the only thing that we had seen of any value was some professional wrestling. The television sets were pretty small; and yet, it was really exciting!

One day Jimmy and Paul knocked on my door and told me that

they had something to show me in Jimmy's garage. We went over to Jimmy's garage and Paul pointed to the patent leather purse and told me to open it up. I naively walked over and opened the purse, and I surely didn't expect to see feces—it looked like human feces. I dropped it and said something like any ten-year-old, "Holy balls; who shit in the purse?"

"You just never mind," Paul said. I had never seen anything like that in my life. I asked them how they had done it, and they just grinned and said in unison, "You ask too many questions, Nathan." Those two looked like Mutt and Jeff, but they sounded like twins when they talked in unison.

Paul and Jimmy had schemed up a plan for the patent leather purse. There was an east-west street that ran by our house on the north side that was named Brownsdale Avenue. I guess the street was so named because if you followed it east about five miles and then a little north, you arrived at a small town named Brownsdale. This street was very busy because most of the trucks hauling animals to the meatpacking plant for slaughter drove along that road to get to the George A. Hormel Meat Packing Plant. All three of our dads worked there, along with a few thousand other souls.

We lived only about a mile east of that meat packing plant. Also, a lot of the employees who lived on the eastern and southern parts of town drove back and forth to work on Brownsdale Avenue. It was a busy road, however, even though there was just a single traffic lane going in each direction.

The great plan that Jimmy and Paul had dreamed up was to place that beautiful feces-filled patent-leather purse out on that Brownsdale Avenue and see if anyone would stop to pick it up.

I honestly cannot remember how many drivers stopped to pick up that purse, and we watched it all from our hiding place in some nearby thick spruce trees. One time two guys raced around the block in pursuit of the black patent leather purse. We were pretty certain that one of the drivers in hot pursuit was a grandson of the founder of the meat packing plant. The "grandson" picked up the purse and started to drive off in a big fancy Lincoln and then slammed on the brakes and exclaimed, "It's shit! It's human shit." He threw the purse out the window and sped off. We thought it was pretty funny to see that rich guy in a fancy car take the bait.

All but one of the purse suckers threw it out of their car window with some very loud cursing. One person never threw it away and so we were back to the dump looking for another purse. Eventually, we got bored with that trick; and anyway, we were a lot less successful with fabric purses than the great black patent-leather purse. Although, I was asked to help contribute to the contents of the patent leather purse, it was beyond my comprehension and participation. The year was 1950. We didn't have television sets yet, so we had to create our own fun. And so it was that we created our own entertainment with the patent leather purse.

(Authors note: Jimmy and Paul both became successful businessmen and Delbert became and is a world-class organist.)

Goliath

One summer day Jimmy, Paul, and I were rummaging through the small woods in the field across from our house. There was a huge wind-damaged branch dangling from an old elm tree. Paul said that it probably happened from high winds or maybe even lightening. Either option sounded plausible to me; I thought Paul was really smart. Jimmy just stood there and stared at that tree with the dangling branch, and then he told us to wait there because he was going home to get a saw. Paul and I sat down with our backs to the tree and waited for Jimmy to come back with a carpenter's handsaw. It was about ten minutes later when Jimmy came back with a saw.

Jimmy was able to shimmy up that tree; and after a few unsuccessful attempts by Paul, we were able to throw the saw up to him. We only waited about fifteen minutes for Jimmy to saw that lame branch from that wind-blown old elm. Then Jimmy triumphantly climbed down from the tree and exclaimed that we now had the makings for a giant slingshot. I couldn't visualize it at that point and Jimmy patiently showed me where he would make some cuts. Then, I could visualize it, but I said, "What will we do with it?"

Paul and Jimmy just looked at me with great big grins and said in unison to the new kid on the block, "You'll see, Nathan. You'll see."

After all of the smaller branches had been cut off, it did look like a giant slingshot. I had a hunch that they had both been looking and talking about a project like this for some time before I had moved into the neighborhood earlier that summer. It was close to lunchtime so we left for home with the understanding that we would meet back there after lunch. I heard Jimmy ask Paul to bring the digger when he came back. And Paul had responded that he would be back as soon as the coast was clear and his mother was taking an afternoon nap.

31

When I got back to the slingshot site after lunch, Jimmy was proudly holding aloft an old rubber car tire tube that he had found in his dad's garage. We would have to cut that tube up to build the greatest slingshot ever assembled. Jimmy and I had waited for a long time after lunch before we had spied Paul coming with something balancing on his shoulder. Jimmy told me that it was a post-hole digger that Paul's dad had used to put in a fence around their yard. Paul was huffing and puffing when he arrived, and I wasn't really sure if he was really out of breath or faking it. That guy was a pretty good actor.

While we had been waiting for Paul to return, Jimmy and I had been looking for the right place to install the greatest kids' weapon on the whole east side of town. We needed a place where we could sling our artillery without tree interference and yet, a place that would not be real visible to the public. Such a place was not to be found in these small woods. We would have to dig the hole out in the open and take our chances of being discovered. Discovered by whom, I wasn't certain. Who was the enemy?

Since Jimmy was the tallest of the three of us, he was the first to start turning the post-hole digger into the ground. It was hard work and a slow process and we figured that we would need to stick this y-shaped branch about three feet into the ground for the best sling-shot technology. I was a pretty short kid so I didn't get a chance to use the digger until we had dug down about a foot into the ground. When my turn came, I soon found out that turning that post-hole digger into the ground wasn't as much fun as it had appeared to be. I decided that afternoon that I didn't want a job as a post-hole digger. We all discovered that digging holes was hard work and we got awful thirsty. Paul had an old army canteen that he had brought with him, and we each took a swig from it without even wiping off the top. Friends didn't worry about germs and anyway guys in war never wiped off the top of a canteen. I didn't particularly like the metal taste of warm water out of that canteen, but I recall it kind of quenched my thirst. And, after-all, we were buddies on a mission.

By early afternoon, we had the sling-shot hole about three feet deep; and we placed the tree limb into the hole. Paul sent me home to get a short two-by-four piece of lumber from our garage (I hoped that my dad wouldn't miss it). We used the two-by-four to pack the dirt into the hole as we filled the hole back up with dirt around the limb.

I got an idea that if this baby worked, we could go around town building them for other kids and maybe make a few bucks. I knew that the guys in my old neighborhood would love to have one of those babies. Paul and Jimmy just laughed at my idea, which made me think that maybe they weren't so smart after all.

When we had the hole filled and packed to the top, I was amazed that the darn limb was pretty rigid. The three of us walked around and admired our efforts. Before we left the site, we camouflaged our new creation to make it less obvious to the traffic along Brownsdale Avenue. The next day, we would meet at Jimmy's garage to make the sling.

Before I went to sleep that night, I remembered a Sunday school story about David and Goliath. I thought that David had a hand-held slingshot model and that he would really be envious of the model that we were making over in the vacant field. I was tired from the long day of work and sleep came easily.

The next morning, we met at Jimmy's garage to make the rubber sling. Jimmy cut the old car tire inner tube into two strips about two inches wide and two feet long. Paul had brought a huge car tire inner tube patch; I'd say about four by four inches square to serve as a pouch. Paul made a hole on each side of the "pouch" with a big spike nail. Making holes in each end of the tire inner tube proved to be more difficult because the rubber would retract back to its normal state. Finally, with a nail, a hole-punch, and a pocketknife we had accomplished our task. After the holes were in place, we secured the pouch to the rubber strips with some old raw-hide shoe laces. We were now ready to tie the rubber strips to the buried tree limb.

I told both of the guys the story about David and Goliath. Since David slew Goliath with a small hand-held slingshot, I wondered what kinds of slewing we would be doing. Furthermore, I suggested that we name our new weapon Goliath, in memory of David, as well as having our own secret code word for our project. They agreed, and Goliath was born.

We then went over to the launch site to attach the rubber strips to Goliath. This would be a trial only since we were out in broad daylight. If the cops had driven by and had seen us, all of our work would have been like water down the drain. Jimmy and I stood in front of the buried limb, blocking the view from passing motorists, about one hundred feet from Brownsdale Avenue, while Paul attached the rubber ends of the sling to the two nubs of the "Y."

It was a sight to behold. We each took a few turns of pulling back the empty pouch and letting it go. I could imagine a small rock going four blocks in the air, but all the empty pouch did was go *whap*. We decided to give it a trial run that night. Before we left the site, we went into the woods and got some more brush to hide Goliath. Golly, I remember feeling how good it felt to be with my new pals, and I was beginning to like that new neighborhood more and more.

One of our neighbors was the director of parks and recreation for the city of Austin, and he always had some extra sports equipment in his garage. We had a good relationship with him, and he let us borrow extra city sports equipment that he kept on hand for our recreational purposes. None of us played tennis, but there were some tennis balls in cans in one of the boxes in his garage. After we had bothered him previously on a number of occasions at night, he had finally given us permission to just take what we needed for equipment and then return it when we were done. He was a neat old guy who was probably in his fifties. He reminded me a lot of my grandpa Frank, a carpenter/contractor, who parked his car by touch and sound. By the scrapings on the neighbor's big old car and on the sides of his single car garage, it appeared to us that he parked by touch too. He and Grandpa Frank were not concerned about the appearance of their cars nor garages.

I could hardly eat dinner that night because I wanted to get back to Goliath for some action. From our kitchen window, you could see the area about one block away. It seemed like darkness would never come, and it never really did get dark in the summer until after I was normally in bed. I convinced my mother that I should stay out after dark because Jimmy, Paul, and I were going out to steal a few green apples from some distant neighbors. Although my mother was a devout Christian, she had a taste for green apples that approached Adam's in the Garden of Eden. I never was certain what the "forbidden fruit" was. Anyway, she gave me her permission to go and not to forget one or two apples for her. I told myself that I had to remember to bring home a couple of green apples to make my story believable. I took a small salt shaker with me as proof that we were going out to "steal" apples.

The three of us met behind my garage and I went over to the neighbor's garage and got two cans of tennis balls, three per can. We decided that Paul would get to fire the first volley. He took the tennis balls and set out for ol' Goliath. Jimmy and I went in the other direction about one block and sat on a lawn right across the street from a cop's house.

We had been sitting there for about fifteen minutes swatting mosquitoes and we were wondering if Paul was having trouble with Goliath. All of a sudden a tennis ball came bouncing down the street. Jimmy and I jumped up for joy and could not believe it. Jimmy got me to sit down and gave me a brief lecture about being cool and not acting like we knew what was going on. I thought, *Who would know what we were jumping and hooting about?*

Then we saw a ball come ricocheting off of the cop's house and we just froze. Within a few seconds, Cliff, the cop, came out of his house and was standing on his steps when another ball hit and bounced down the street. Jimmy said the cop was watching us; but when his house got hit and we were just sitting there in his view, he knew that we hadn't done it. I was petrified! Jimmy told me to get up and nonchalantly walk the opposite way from where Paul was launching the tennis balls.

We hadn't walked more than about twenty feet when we heard another house being hit. We kept walking. Another neighbor came outside and we heard him yell to the cop, "Hey Cliff, what's going on?" The cop yelled back that he thought it was raining tennis balls. Jimmy and I laughed and I said, "I wonder where they're coming from?"

We circled around the block and headed toward Goliath, and I quickly slipped into an unsuspecting neighbor's yard and swiped a couple of apples for my mom. Paul came running down the alley and he was all out of breath.

"I fired all six of them; did you see any?"

We told him that we heard or saw four of them hit and that two of them had hit the cop's house. We also told him that it was really cool to be sitting there as innocent as could be. We then decided that we had really had a successful night, and we would look for the tennis balls in the morning. The next morning when we were walking around looking for the tennis balls, we saw a cop car going up and down the streets. We decided to stay away from Goliath. In our brief search, we only found two tennis balls.

A short time later, we were sitting in my yard looking at some old comic books and drinking cool aid. A cop car pulled up by the field where our mammoth Goliath was planted. Two big cops got out of their car and walked over to the site and began rocking our pride and joy back and forth. They pulled it out of the ground and carried it over and put it into their trunk of their police car. They tied the trunk down and sped off with Goliath sticking partially out of their trunk.

Jimmy and I never did get our turns, but then Paul never got to see the end result as we had. We were really glad those cops never figured out whose handy work it had been. Too bad that Goliath got confiscated, because we had some real plans for later that summer of 1950 when we could get bigger apples off the trees. They would have been great for launching.

Paul said that he wondered how the stupid cops had found out about Goliath. I figured they were just lucky and Jimmy agreed. We never saw Goliath again.

The Shaw Gym for Boys

There was once a building on the north end of Main Street in Austin, Minnesota, which was known as the Shaw Gym for Boys. The Shaw Gym was built in 1924 with funds provided by Mr. Oliver W. Shaw and given to the Austin Library Board. The Shaw Gym was dedicated in October, 1925. Mr. Shaw was the first president of Austin's First National Bank, founded in 1868, and he served as its president for fifty years. Shaw Elementary School in Austin was also named after Mr. Oliver W. Shaw.

The Shaw Gym housed a regulation-sized basketball court with seating in a balcony above the floor and in the lower level handball courts, several regulation pool and table tennis tables, a boxing ring and work-out area for amateurs, and a shower and locker room area. All of the facilities were available free to the boys and men in Austin, and the facility was run by the City Park and Recreation Board during the fifties. There was an occasional teenage dance held in the gym and that was, as I recall, the only co-ed function held there.

Two of my brothers, Raymond and David, had gone to the facility for several years prior to 1951. One had to be twelve years old in order to get a membership card and use the facilities. I wanted to join so badly that I lied about my age in the summer of '51 (I was eleven) and got my first membership card.

Old men, by my definition, were the supervisors of the Shaw Gym; and they strictly enforced the rules. No rowdy behavior was permitted. If a pool ball jumped the table, the player responsible got a hole punched in his membership card. With gray concrete painted-floors, it was obvious when a pool ball left the table and went bouncing merrily away. With three punches, as I recall, you were suspended for a number of days and given a stern lecture. The lecture was the worst part, and there were very few repeat offenders. I never got more than one punch the whole four years that I played pool and table tennis down there.

I won two pool tournaments in my age bracket in 1953 and 1954 and two table tennis tournaments in 1954 and 1955 at the Shaw Gym. By the time I was fifteen, I was too involved in high school athletics and other school activities to spend much time at the Shaw Gym. It was a wonderful facility for wholesome recreation, and I'm certain that it kept many boys from getting into mischief.

The Shaw Gym closed in 1980 due to lack of sufficient funds for repair of the facility, and it was razed in 1983. I have many fine memories of the Shaw Gym, but all that physically remains today is a vacant lot next to Brick's Furniture Store in Austin.

At my age I still consider myself better-than-average with a pool cue or a table tennis paddle. And, although my eyes and coordination are not what they once were, I can still play table tennis competitively for a couple of hours in my age group. Those two recreational activities have been lifetime sports for me and probably never would have happened if it had not been for the Shaw Gym.

David's Eastside Paper Route

My brother David had a daily paper route on the east side of Austin with over ninety deliveries of the *Austin Daily Herald*. Sometimes, I would go with him to pick up the papers hot-off-the-press downtown. We would stand by the benches and roll the papers up and stuff them into his canvas bag and ride back home on our bikes to begin the delivery. With all of that fresh newsprint, we would have ink all over our hands so we were careful not to touch our faces or clothing until we could wash our hands.

Often David would let me call on the customers and collect payment from his customers. This was a weekly event and very few people paid in advance for the paper. As I recall, it cost about thirty-five cents a week for home delivery. When I did the collection for David, he said I could keep the tips. Tips were few and far between, except at Christmas time; and then it was not unusual for us to get ten to fifteen boxes of chocolate-covered cherries. To this day, I cannot go near a chocolate-covered cherry.

One Saturday morning when I was collecting, I stopped at an old bachelor's house who always seemed to pay in advance. He wanted to pay a month in advance so he tried to give me a two-dollar bill. To pay a month in advance would have been one dollar and forty cents, and he said I could keep the change. It was the first time that I had collected from him; but I wasn't any dummy. He was not going to fool this eleven-year-old. I refused to take the two-dollar bill because I had never seen one before and so I didn't think it was real. He tried unsuccessfully to convince me that it was good. Finally, he found a dime and a quarter and paid for one week.

When I got home and told David how the bachelor had tried to dupe me he just sighed and said, "Nathan, that two-dollar bill was real money that you turned down and you lost a sixty-cent tip." That tip would have been worth five admissions to the movies at that time. I never made that mistake again.

Painting for Uncle Bob

My Uncle Bob gave me my first job at thirteen years of age. He hired me to paint the picket fence that enclosed his back yard. I'd estimate that it was approximately two hundred lineal feet in length and about three-and-a-half feet high. It was badly in need of paint, and I had never really painted anything but a rusty old red wagon prior to that.

I arose early one June morning in 1953, wiped the dew off of my bicycle seat, and rode across town. Uncle Bob and Aunt Beverly were really special to me. When Uncle Bob returned home after World War II, he brought each of us bright blue silk jackets with our names written in Chinese and English. I was so proud of that jacket that I literally wore it out.

When I arrived at Uncle Bob's house, he invited me in for milk and cookies. Uncle Bob worked at the Hormel meat packing plant, but he had also picked up carpentry skills from his carpenter/contractor father, my Grandpa Frank. So Uncle Bob built homes when he wasn't working at the plant. The first thing that Uncle Bob showed me was how to scrape off the old peeling paint. That wasn't any fun at all and I wondered when we would get to painting the fence. What we decided to do was scrape about a twenty-foot section and then paint it. Uncle Bob showed me how to stir up the white paint and demonstrated how to paint a couple of the pickets. Then he watched me paint a couple of the pickets, praised me for how quickly I had caught on, and left for work.

Aunt Beverly would come out every once in a while and give me encouragement. She also made lunch for me, and I had discovered that painting the four sides of a picket fence was a slow-moving process. About four o'clock in the afternoon, Aunt Beverly told me that I had done enough for that day and that I could resume work the next day. She had said that I was a regular Tom Sawyer, although I wasn't quite sure what she meant by that. I told myself that I would ask my mother what that meant when I got home. I had completed just a little over one third of the picket fence that first day.

The next day was Saturday and I rode my bike back over to Uncle Bob's house to resume my painting of the picket fence. About 11:30 in the morning, I ran out of paint. Bev said that Bobby would be home for lunch shortly and he would get me some more paint. I went back outside and sat under the shade of a sprawling Maple tree. When Bobby came home for lunch, he called the paint store and told them that I would be down shortly to pick up the paint. I thought that it would be a chore trying to carry the paint and ride my bike at the same time.

Bobby hung up the phone and said to me, "Have you ever driven a car, Nathan?"

I wasn't expecting a question like that so I lied and said, "Yah, a couple of times out at my cousin Burton's farm."

Then Bobby said, "The keys are in the ol' Pontiac (*a '41 model* I thought) outside. Take it down to Hardy's Paint and Wallpaper store and get the paint I ordered."

I just froze right there in my spot. This was a dream come true. Bobby followed up his last statement with, "You do know where Hardy's store is, don't you?" Uncle Bob was about twenty-eight years old at that time. I responded that I knew exactly where the store was.

I went out to the car and found an old pillow in the back seat to sit on, since I was barely five feet tall. I could just barely reach the clutch, brake pedals, and accelerator. Luckily the car started okay, and I set off driving jerkily for the first time. Wow, it was something to behold! Each time I stopped at a stop sign it was a new experience. Two different times, I killed the car. It was shear luck when I had left the house in a rather smooth fashion. I sat as tall as I could for a boy of thirteen, with a pillow beneath me, and made every effort I could to look older. I grabbed an old blue and white striped railroad-type cap lying on the front seat and put it on. That cap would make me look a lot older, I was certain.

I remember thinking, *If only my friends could see me now driving down the street all by myself.* I figured no cops would stop a guy just driving down town, a guy with an engineer's cap on. They'd probably think it was just a guy who just got done working at the railroad and was on his way to Lefty's Bar, on the east side of town.

I parked the car by St. Olaf Lutheran Church, which was just around the corner from the paint store. There were a lot of vacant parking places there and I didn't have a clue on how one went about parking a car between two other cars. My Grandpa Frank parked his car by touch. First he'd bang into the car in front of him and then he'd bang into the car behind him until he thought the car was in about the right place. Needless-to-say, my grandpa's car always had a lot of bumps and bruises. I hoped and prayed that nobody would park in front of me while I was at the paint store.

John Hardy, a kid whom I had met during my past year in seventh grade was in the store with his mom waiting on customers. I told him that I had driven down there by myself in my uncle's car and parked it over by St. Olaf Church. He just looked at me and said, "Johnson, you really know how to bullshit." (He said that right in front of his mother.)

"Honest, John, watch me when I leave and you'll see I'm telling the truth."

I signed for the two gallons of paint and swaggered out the door engineer cap and all. John was right behind me and was being a smart-ass about my cap. As I pulled away from the church, I looked quickly in the rear-view mirror and there was John back about two hundred feet away slapping his leg and hooting. He would be my proof when I told some of my friends about my first driving experience. When I got back to Uncle Bob's, he wanted to know if everything had gone okay; and I assured him that everything had gone just fine, real "hunky-dory."

I finished painting the fence on the following Monday morning. To my dismay, Bobby had told me that one coat of paint just did not seem to cover very well, and I set about painting it again. By Thursday afternoon, I had completely painted the fence twice. Bob and Beverly were very pleased with my work on the picket fence and paid me with six two-dollar bills. Although I had vowed to myself never to paint another picket fence, that thought faded as I tucked those two-dollar bills into my pocket. I knew from my paper route experience that there were two-dollar bills. I had made twelve bucks in less than a week and driven a car by myself downtown. I was flying high as I rode my bike home.

Wednesday night, Uncle Bob called and talked to my dad and I heard my dad say that it would be okay with him if I wanted to do it. My dad then handed the phone to me and Uncle Bob asked me if I wanted to paint his house. He told me that he would paint the high parts on the one-and-a-half story house, and I would paint the rest. When I was done painting the house, he would pay me 25 dollars. I was ecstatic in my response of yes.

It took me a little over two weeks because of rain delays to finish painting Uncle Bob's house a medium-shade green. I also got to run two more errands with his car. On one of those errands, I saw one of my best friends Georgey-Porgy on his bike; and I could see that he was as green as the house I was painting — he was "green-with-envy."

The house and the picket fence looked really nice with their fresh coats of paint. I was proud of my accomplishments. I thought of myself as a Tom Sawyer; my mother had clued me in about some of Mark Twain's writing.

I bought a new swimming suit and a new pair of shoes and saved the rest of my earnings to buy school clothes in August. I also spent a couple of bucks on illegal firecrackers from one of the notorious east-side neighborhood boys. It was great having some spending money.

On the Farm

Burton and Dorothy Kettelson own a one hundred sixty acre farm approximately eight miles northwest of Austin, Minnesota, and about a quarter mile west of Corning, Minnesota. When they were still actively farming, before they semi-retired and began renting out their land, they had some livestock; but mostly they were small grain farmers in some of the richest soil in the world. Their crops consisted primarily of corn, oats, and soy beans. They raised four beautiful daughters and have always been Christian people attending Red Oak Grove Lutheran Church about half way between Corning and Blooming Prairie, Minnesota. This is the same church where my farm-boy dad, Wilburn M. "Ted" Johnson attended and also where he was baptized and later confirmed in about 1927. Dorothy was the daughter of Mildred, my dad's sister, so she is my cousin.

My brother Ray, who was four years older than I, had worked on Burton and Dorothy's farm a few years before me; and they were always high on praise for Ray's work. That was prior to the summer of 1954, the summer that I, as a fourteen-year-old was "farmed" out to Burton and Dorothy. I am reasonably certain that my dad thought it would be a good experience for a city-boy, and I was pretty certain at that time that Burton thought I was kind of a smart-alecky slouch.

Although we had frequently visited several of my relatives' farms, I had never stayed overnight with any of my cousins. The nature of daily farm work was pretty much a mystery to me other than reading and a few field trips in school. Oh, to be sure, there was always lots of talk about farming at family reunions between the elders, but seldom with us kids. Work on the farm was seldom talked about by my farm cousins. And, when my dad talked about working on the farm when he was a kid, I thought his stories had occurred a hundred years ago. It was

45

hard for me to relate to farming with horses as my dad had done.

At home I was generally up by 7:30 in the morning, which was pretty early according to my neighborhood city friends. On the farm, we were usually up by 6:15 a.m. One of my jobs early in the morning was to go out in the pasture and bring in the cows for milking. That was one of the jobs that I hated the most because I did not like walking out through the pasture and getting my pants wet up to my knees for a bunch of stupid cows. Once I got them back to the barn, it was up to Burt to get them milked and the milk stored for pick up. I was not amused by Burton when he would occasionally grab one of the cow's udders and squirt me with warm milk. I thought it was rude and the milk was sticky, and to make it worse, Burton always laughed.

Burton had Minneapolis Moline and Allis Chalmers tractors, but what their horsepower was, I just don't recall. Farmers always know what the horsepower is. I do recall that once I had learned how to drive the Allis tractor, he let me take it into Corning to pick up some supplies. Knowing when to let out the clutch was a real test for me in the beginning. There were also some break levers between the seat and the rear wheels, which presented some real challenges. If you pulled on the lever to the left, the tractor would turn to the left on a dime. I had tried this on a few occasions when Burton wasn't around, and I had nearly lost control of the machine. I decided that I didn't need to know how to use those brakes. I would rely on the steering wheel.

One of the field chores over the course of that summer on the farm was harvesting oats. On Burton's farm, that meant I would drive the tractor while pulling a piece of machinery that would cut the oats behind us. Burton would ride and operate that equipment. The cutting-machinery required that I have the left-rear tractor tire right next to the oats to be cut. My depth perception was not very good since I refused to wear eye glasses because I thought they detracted from my appearance. After I had stopped the tractor by Burt yelling at me and after receiving several lectures from him, he came up with a plan. We disconnected the cutting machine from the tractor and went back to the farm yard. Burton found an old broom stick and cut it off so that he could tie it around the front axle so that it would protrude the same distance as the rear tire. That way I could drive the tractor and keep the end of the broom handle at the edge of the oats to be cut. Burton's plan worked very well.

There was an old Chevy on their farm. Although it was not old in years, it was in appearance and Burton let me drive it once in awhile around the farm yard or out to one of the fields. I felt pretty good about that since I was still another year away from getting a permit to drive with a licensed person. I was a pretty thin fourteen-year-old, probably five-foot-four and one hundred and twenty-five pounds. During that summer, I believed that I was beginning to develop some muscle.

It was common-place for neighbors to share manpower, combines, plows, balers, and other equipment so that each farmer didn't have to purchase them all. There was an occasion that summer after we had finished combining oats that we helped a neighbor across the road in a process called threshing. The threshing machine was huge and was powered by a high-powered tractor, with a long continuous running belt off of its power-takeoff. The power-takeoff at the center of the rear of the tractor was a spinning cylinder that spun the leather belt to the threshing machine. That belt powered the machinery to separate the oats from the chaff. The oats went into a huge hopper and the chaff was blown outside the threshing machine in a big pile. Chaff blowing in the air on a hot July day and then sticking to the worker's skin and clothing made for a truly uncomfortable day.

One of the workers across the road was mentally challenged, but was a physical specimen. Freddy could talk a little, but seldom chose to. Freddy wore bib-top overhauls and his biceps and forearms rippled with muscles. He had short hair, concealed by an old sweat-stained cap, and a smile that nearly went from ear to ear. From his bow-legged walk, I could sense that there was tremendous power in his legs.

There were always three or four of us young men who would ride on a hayrack pulled by a tractor out into the field to pick up oat shocks. After the oats had been cut, there was a machine that would pick up the oats and tie it in bundles. The bundles would be stacked vertically in a form shaped like an "Indian Tepee" so that they would stay dry until picked up. Those vertical bundles were called shocks and usually consisted of eight of the bundles.

Once we got out to the field, we would use our pitch forks to take a part of a shocked bundle and toss it onto the hayrack. When it appeared that the hayrack was full, we would take it back in to the threshing machine. On one of our hayrack rides that day when we were out in the field, one of the other young men kept challenging Freddy to stick his pitchfork into a whole shock and throw it over a full load. I couldn't pick up a whole shock on one pitchfork, let alone pick it up and throw it over the entire load. That would be impossible! Freddy jammed his pitchfork into the pile and with a tremendous grunt pitched that entire shock over the full hayrack. That's the truth.

Although the Kittlesons had running water and an inside toilet, they did not have a shower, as I recall. I think after some time that I was beginning to stink and Dorothy suggested that I take a shower. I refused to take a bath in their bath tub. Burton rigged up a shower outside using a garden hose at one inside-corner of the house. I was a pretty private guy and I was afraid that Dorothy or one of the girls would see me nude. You can believe that I didn't spend a whole lot of time in that cold water shower. I remember that I did feel refreshed after it was all over.

Another unique item at the Kittelsons was their wall phone. The part that you spoke into was attached to the wall part of the phone and the listening device was on a cord about two-feet long and attached to the wall box. I was never quite certain when the phone rang if I should pick it up or not. They were on a party line, and I wasn't sure if their ring was two short rings and one long ring, or one long and two short rings. Therefore, I seldom answered the phone.

Two other chores are worth mentioning at this time. Even worse than going after the cows in the morning, was cleaning manure out of the barn. It was hard work although we didn't do it very often. Baling hay was a terribly hot job too and grabbing the bales as they came out of the baling machine and stacking them on the hay rack was always a challenge. The fields were bumpy and loose hay blowing and sticking to your hot sweaty body made the afternoon breaks pure joy. Dorothy would bring us out wonderful sandwiches, cookies, and cool drinks. She was a great cook.

Burton and Dorothy paid me 45 dollars for that summer's work and they may have overpaid me dollar-wise in their minds, but I learned immeasurable lessons that summer. August came and it was time for me to go home and get prepared for school. I worried that my school and neighborhood friends that I had known before the farm experience would be gone. They were not. Dorothy and Burton played an important part in the development of Nathan's footprints.

Two Teachers

I have had the good fortune of having many outstanding associations with teachers and educators in my life. At this time, I want to briefly share with you just two of those teachers who had profoundly different impacts upon me during my freshman year at Austin High School.

Frank W. Bridges

Mr. Frank W. Bridges was my freshman high school English teacher. Mr. Bridges many years later, after my army discharge, was also my college freshman speech teacher at Austin Community College (the name has since been changed to Riverland Community College and their new theatre building was dedicated in his honor).

Mr. Bridges, in that high school freshman English class, gave me an appreciation for literature and theatre that remain with me to this day. One of the plays that we read that freshman year was Shakespeare's, *Merchant of Venice*.

Frank Bridges is a handsome and charming man; and as a teacher, had a serious, but friendly teaching style. He had a major influence on my choices of speech and English as majors and minors in my college undergraduate degree. Mr. Bridges is retired now and still resides in Austin. He has always been a gentleman, and I'm pleased to have known him and to have been a student of his. He was an excellent teacher!

Jeanne Cleary

One day in March, between the end of winter sports and the beginning of spring sports of my freshman year in high school, I was approached by Ms. Jeanne Cleary, a girl's physical education teacher. Ms. Cleary was always enthusiastic and friendly. She said that high school girls had told her that very few boys danced at school or community dances. She also said that the girls told her that because the boys wouldn't or couldn't dance, often times the girls danced to the new rock and roll with other girls. I said that was true. Furthermore, I told her that once in a while that some of us would dance with the girls to the slow numbers. We didn't know how to dance to the rock and roll.

Then she said, "Nathan, if you'll get five-to-ten boys after school, I'll get the girls, a record player, some forty-five rpm rock and roll records and we'll teach you how to dance." It was a challenge and an offer that I could not refuse. Two days later, I showed up with seven of my buddies prepared for the worst. We had about three lessons of approximately forty-five minutes each and we were ready to go.

Although we were a little reluctant at the first few dances after the lessons, we got better and better. Instead of going to dances and leaning against the wall as we had in the past, we started asking girls to dance. Words can not adequately describe to you the dramatic impact that being able to dance had on our social lives. It was wonderful! Those dancing lessons remain with me to this day. With some major and some minor adjustments, I've used the "Lindy" to adapt to the various music styles that have occurred over the past forty-five years. "Jeanne, you saw an opportunity to teach and you did it! Thank you for that kind gesture."

Bowling Balls and "Bushwhacking"

There were some boys in my sophomore class that played some dirty tricks on unsuspecting people. I think that when they were by themselves they were pretty decent guys, but when they got together they did some strange things.

One night during the spring of my sophomore year, I was sitting on a short ledge in front of the Leothold-Peterson clothing store on the main street of Austin. That store was next to a store called Nemitz, which still exists today and is run by Gary Nemitz, a grandson of the founder. One could play pool at Nemitz's, buy all kinds of newspapers and magazines, and buy cigarettes and fine cigars. I don't recall ever seeing a woman or girl in that downstairs store in the fifties.

Anyway, I was sitting on the ledge when a car with three of the "rowdies" that I mentioned above stopped and asked me if I wanted to join them. I asked them what they were up to, and they responded that they were just cruising around looking for "chicks." I joined them.

After they picked me up, they went north on main street and stopped in the middle of a small bridge over the Cedar River, and two of them jumped out and opened the trunk. I recall asking the driver what they were after and he said they had just been out to Echo Lanes, a local bowling alley. Apparently, when some of the men had finished bowling, they would move over to the lounge in Echo Lanes and have a couple of beers. The men would leave their bowling balls tucked securely in their bowling bags, along with their shoes, near the ball racks in the bowling alley.

Prior to picking me up, those three guys had gone out to the bowling alley, walked in and each picked up one of the bowling ball bags and walked out undisturbed. I was shocked because I knew that my dad had bowled in a league at Echo Lanes that night. Did they steal his ball? I had no way of knowing. In a matter of seconds, they had pitched the bowling bags over the side of the bridge into the water with three noticeable splashes, *kerplunk-kerplunk-kerplunk!* The water was probably only about fifteen feet deep below the bridge.

The boys got back into the car all excited and proud of their latest endeavor and wanted to go back to the bowling alley for another stupid episode of stealing bowling balls. I told them that I wasn't interested and that my dad was probably still out there, although I was pretty certain that he wasn't. My dad would not have stayed after bowling on a week night because he had to be to work by 6:30 a.m. and he was a dedicated worker. Anyway, the whole idea of what they had done scared me, and I thought we could probably have been arrested if we had gotten caught.

One of the guys suggested that we go out in the country and go "bushwhacking." In Austin that meant that you went looking for teenagers parked out in the country and tried to sneak up on them in the dark and scare them. I had only done that twice before with some other guys and we hadn't been very successful. That night would be totally different.

We drove out into the country side and one of the guys spotted a car parked a long way up the road. The driver turned off the car lights, and we drove for awhile in the dark very slowly. You could hear the gravel on the road crunching as the car crept down the road. Then Greg, who academically was near the top of our class of four hundred, stopped the car. I was told by Roger, a future big-time division-one athlete, to go with him; and we slipped down into the ditch and started running on our approach to the car. Roger told me that the other two guys were doing the same thing in the ditch on the other side of the road. When we got even with the car, Roger told me to lie down. I remember asking when we were going to rush the car. He told me just to lie there and be quiet. All we could hear were crickets chirping, and I wasn't very comfortable with that operation and the grass was long and full of dew. The mosquitoes were fierce and I was lying there getting wet and thinking that I should have stayed sitting on the ledge down town when it happened.

In the stillness of that night, there were two tremendous blasts followed by screaming and Roger said to me, "Haul ass!" We were running down the ditch and I was yelling at him trying to get answers to what had happened. He told me he would tell me in the car. Running in the dark, I tripped over a rock and took a dive into the long grass and dirt. *How would I explain my soiled clothes to my mom?* When we got into the car, Greg quickly got it started and maneuvered it around so that we could take off in the opposite direction. With the back wheels spinning and spitting gravel against the underside of the car and hurling the rest back behind us, we were gone.

What I didn't know was that one of the guys who went down the other side of the ditch had a twelve-gauge double-barrel shotgun. What had happened, according to Roger, was that they had sneaked up beside that car, laid the barrel of that shotgun across the hood of the car in the direction of where Roger and I were lying, and had fired off two shots. With the noise and the visual fire-power of those two shots, the couple in the car started screaming. I don't blame them; I would have done the same. I never did find out who was in that car, I never went with those guys again, and I never went bushwhacking again. And, that's the truth.

Blowing the Whistle

The George A. Hormel Company blew a whistle that could be heard for miles at noon and 1 p.m. There was in the 1950s a jewelry store on Main Street in Austin, Minnesota, that had a large clock in the front window of the store. I've been told that the "whistle-blower" would walk past the jewelry store and set his pocket watch by that clock. At precisely the correct time the "whistle-blower" would blow the packing plant whistle. When the clerk in the jewelry store heard the whistle, she would set the clock in the window. Believe it or not.

Hazing or Kidnapping?

There was a tradition among junior and senior males at Austin High School that had occurred every spring for years, and we called it "hazing." In legal language, both then and now, it would be defined as kidnapping. In the "hazing" that was the Austin tradition, it was meant to be pretty harmless, at least that's the way it had been. So in the spring of 1956, testosterone flowed freely and teenage boys seemed destined to prove their manliness and immaturity at the same time.

This is how it worked in Austin. In late April or early May, senior boys would ride around at night in cars looking for junior boys who might be walking by themselves. They would park in inconspicuous places by the library, by restaurants, by girlfriends' homes, by athletic contests, and the like. Once a "victim" was spotted, several boys would pile out of the car, chase down the "junior enemy," grab him, and bring him back to the car. Then they would put him in the back seat of the car and drive him out in the country about a mile and drop him off so he could walk home. The next day in school the "victim" would be telling friends about his capture, and the seniors would be bragging about whom they had "hazed" the night before. The junior boys did the same thing to the senior boys.

As a sophomore in high school, I had a lot of friends that were both juniors and seniors. I also had a lot of friends who were sophomores and freshmen. I decided for hazing purposes that I would join with the senior boys since the current juniors would be the opposition when I became a junior. Past history found very few sophomores involved in the "game of hazing"; and if they were, they had associated themselves with the juniors. Needless to say, my joining forces with the seniors did not go over well with the junior boys. I was always on the alert when I was by myself, and my ace-in-the-hole was that I could run faster than nearly all of the boys who would be potentially chasing me. It was an ego trip for me to be accepted by the senior boys, and they probably thought I was setting myself up for failure.

One of the seniors had a brilliant plan to hide about thirty-five seniors inside the huge tractor tires at the Firestone store on the corner of Main Street and Oakland Avenue in downtown Austin. Part of the plan was to have four senior boys sitting in a decoy parked-car in front of a pool hall called "The Spot," right next door to the Firestone store. I was in the car with three seniors when a car full of juniors drove by and saw us sitting there. Within ten minutes, there were three cars of juniors double-parked and all huddled around our decoy car. They were rocking the car and smarting off in all kinds of ways. Then the driver of the car blasted the horn and all those seniors poured out of those tires like the "Trojan Horse." We jumped out of the car too and we captured seven juniors before they really knew what had happened. It was a beautiful plan and executed with military precision.

As a result of the tractor tire incident and some fight talk in school the next day between two of the participants, they decided to "duke-it-out" in a city park on the south side of town. I'd guess that about one hundred and fifty boys, mostly juniors and seniors, were down in the park the next afternoon for the fight. After the two fighters had bloodied each other's noses, the fight was broken up by some of the senior boys. One of them said, "Why are we fighting each other? We're friends. If we want to fight someone, let's go to Albert Lea." (Albert Lea was an arch rival in high school and city sports and was located about twenty miles west of Austin.) I think that there were over thirty cars and trucks that drove to Albert Lea and arrived there in the early afternoon.

Of course no one in Albert Lea knew that a mob of leaderless teenager boys was going to invade their town so they weren't prepared for it. Upon arrival in Albert Lea, it was complete bedlam. Austin guys were walking down the middle of streets and stopping traffic. I witnessed several boys go into an ice cream parlor in downtown Albert Lea, demand ice cream, cookies, etcetera. and then refuse to pay. I would estimate that a good portion of the downtown business district was "grid-locked." I was with my friend Jim Baldwin, who was one guy who could run faster than me. It was an exciting, but potentially hostile event.

All of a sudden after about thirty minutes of "Austin Party Time," police were everywhere. I saw local police, state police, and deputy sheriffs taking control. They handcuffed a couple guys and put them in a squad car. Jim and I decided to run for his car. Wild Jim wanted to get the guys out of jail, but that didn't seem like a smart thing to do. We were running down alleys, trying to avoid crossing streets and trying to steer clear of the cops. We also ran into friends at every turn. Some police officers had bull-horns and were telling us to get out of town or we would be arrested for disturbing the peace. We ran into a couple of seniors who said they were going to meet with the police to get the guys out who had been taken to jail.

After approximately forty-five minutes, the police on their loud speakers said that if we left town immediately, they would release our friends whom they had detained. We made haste for our car and saw almost all of our classmates doing the same. It was highly exciting, but I was filled with relief as we drove back home to Austin. I was more afraid of what my dad would do to me if he knew what I had been up to, especially if I had been arrested. That ended the hazing for that year.

When we were juniors, hazing was not nearly as exciting. Plus "hazers" were getting more creative and dangerous. Some guys taken out in the country had their shoes taken off, and an event that almost seemed like a "rite-of-passage" now had an evil element to it. One junior boy, a cousin of mine, had been taken across the state line into Iowa, a mere twelve miles away, tied up, and left in a barn. Even sixteen-year-olds recognized that as kidnapping.

By the time we were seniors, the school district passed a policy that said that anyone caught hazing would not graduate from high school. Nobody was willing to take that risk so hazing, as we knew it, came to an end in the spring of 1958.

The Student Council

I was elected and involved in student government from the time I was in elementary school through high school. In the spring of 1957, I decided to run for president of the student council, a position that was coveted by many and required that one be a high school senior.

My campaign chair was a good friend, an enthusiastic promoter, and a fun-loving guy named Ronnie Raasch. He designed and machine-printed triangular-shaped lapel pin-on signs that read, Vote Nate for '58, Nate's Great in '58, and the like. He made machine-printed signs for the hallways in school, and we worked together on home-made banners.

My competitor in that student council election was Mier Wolf, who was much more academic than I. It's probably a good thing that we never had a "political" debate for the office since in my opinion Mier was much more verbally skilled. I presume that it was a close election, but we never knew what the vote tally was because the votes were tallied by teachers and counselors. I suspect that many teachers and the student council advisor, a counselor, would have preferred that Mier would have won. I prevailed, however, and left another footprint at Austin High School.

As a result of being elected student council president, I was enrolled in a one-week leadership training session in late August 1957 held at St. Olaf College in Northfield, Minnesota. Student council presidents attended that training session from all over the state, and it reminded me in some respects of the leadership session that I had attended as a result of being elected Junior Class President. Those sessions were held in St. Paul, as part of the American Legion's Boys State.

A student council president at Austin High School could only participate in one sport as a senior, because of the time constraints of the office. I chose football and ended up making all-conference. As student council president, I was given a study hall over the noon hour with some work table space in the principal's general office area. Mary Dunlop, the elected student council secretary, and I met daily and prepared for council meetings and follow-up activities of the council. It was fun. Also, as a result of being the student council president, I was a student member of the American Red Cross local chapter and attended their meetings.

We probably averaged one general assembly per month during my senior year. We would have guest speakers and all sophomores, juniors, and seniors would be seated in our huge auditorium. As student council president, it was my assignment to introduce the guest speakers or entertainers. I would get a whole lot of information about five minutes before the presentation and then try to condense it into a brief introduction. When I walked onto the stage, there were always a few cute comments yelled at me because most knew I would light-up and blush. There were also built into the stage floor red footlights, which added to my flush. In the school newspaper, *The Senteniel*, in one of the last issues of my senior year, had me willing my "Royal Flush" to the incoming student council president Doug Wright.

Learning basic leadership procedures and conducting meetings would become a way of life for me. Serving as student council president was a valuable leadership experience for me and helped prepare me for many leadership roles in my adult life.

Football's Surprise Victim

I think, as I look back, that head football coach Mr. Art Hass and his assistants Mr. Elton Lerke and Mr. John Stephans, knew that their time for winning had arrived in the fall of 1957. Although we ended the season with an eight and one record and shared the Big Nine Conference title with Rochester, I did not hear the following story until a class reunion twenty-five years later.

During one of the football games in the fall of 1957, one of our tackles told our big end that he was getting "cheap-shots" from one of the Albert Lea High School players.

As recalled by Roger Voss, the six-foot-six end, had told the tackle, Jerry Peterson, "Next time a play is run our way, we'll get him."

I carried the ball the next time that a play went the blocking-route of Roger and Jerry; and there was a big pile-up at the end of the play when I was tackled. I could hear someone cry out in pain as the officials were yelling at us to "un-pile."

As Roger related at the class reunion, "I reached under that pile and I grabbed the Albert Lea guy and just squeezed. " Roger Voss, now six-foot-nine, has huge hands and he said he had trotted back to our huddle with a great deal of satisfaction for helping his buddy Jerry take care of the Albert Lea player.

After the play when we were assembled back in the huddle, Jerry was the last one back. Tears were streaming down his face. In pain Jerry mumbled, "That son-of-a-bitch tried to tear off my balls!"

Instead of getting the Albert Lea player as planned, Roger had grabbed Jerry by mistake and waited twenty-five years to tell us about it. Jerry wasn't at that class reunion. Jerry may not know that Roger was the guy who tried to make him a soprano. According to Roger, it really happened.

(Author's note: Jerry Peterson was selected to the Minnesota All-State Football team in 1957. The Austin High School football field was named in honor of Coach Art Hass at the Austin/Albert Lea Football game on October 9, 2003. It was a well-deserved honor.)

Austin Has Two State Champs

In March of 1958, Austin High School won the state of Minnesota Public High School Basketball Championship. Pacelli High School, a small Catholic high school, located just across the street from Austin High School, won the state private high school basketball championship that same year. Austin High's players were big for that time, and Pacelli's players were smaller and quicker. It would have been fun to have a local playoff between the two state championship teams, but it never occurred.

Washington D.C. and New York City

In April of 1958, I went on a trip with a group of approximately twenty-five senior classmates, out of approximately 375 seniors, and a similar number from Winona High School, located approximately one hundred miles east of Austin. The trip was sponsored by the local YMCA, and we went round-trip by train from Austin to Winona, to Washington D.C. and to New York City on a "Know-Your-Government Seminar" for two weeks. Neither I nor my parents had enough money to finance my trip expenses, approximately 200 dollars, so my dad co-signed for my first loan, which was just about enough for me to go on the trip.

In Washington D. C. we went to all of the tourist attractions including the White House, Washington, Lincoln, and Jefferson monuments, Arlington National Cemetery, the Smithsonian Institute, National Archives, and the like. We also went to sessions of the House and Senate and had a meeting and a photo session with one of our senators, Hubert H. Humphrey. During our stay in Washington, the cherry blossoms bloomed and they were absolutely gorgeous. It was a wonderful educational experience and a real eye-opener to the political world for me.

In New York City, we went to the United Nations building, Empire State Building, Wall Street, the Statute of Liberty, Times Square, and one of the Broadway plays that we saw was *The Ropedancers* featuring Art Carney, who I thought was just a comedian on the Jackie Gleason Show. I was wrong, he was a great actor. We also saw another play called *Bells Are Ringing,* starring Judy Holliday. We saw a performance

63

by the New York Philharmonic Orchestra, conducted by Robert Shaw, and "The Creation," sung by The Robert Shaw Chorale. To name-drop further, we dined in the Russian Tea Room.

One afternoon when we had some free time, we were walking in Times Square and I ran into my Brother David's buddy Skip (Dale Vermilyea) who had enlisted into the navy with him in 1955. I thought at the time what were the odds of running into someone from Austin, Minnesota in New York City on an April day in 1958? For that matter, what would be the odds today?

One night in one of my friend's room in the New York City hotel, we decided to have a sit-up contest with four of us boys involved, two from Winona and two from Austin. The winner would get a penny for each sit-up completed more than the other three contestants. We drew straws, and I was the first one to compete. I don't think that I had ever done more than sixty sit-ups prior to that day and hardly any for a couple of months. Being first, I decided that I would give those other three guys something to shoot at. I strained myself to use my last ounce of energy, and I completed one hundred forty-six sit-ups without anyone holding down my ankles. The other three guys were so impressed that they conceded the match and each paid me one dollar and forty-six cents. I was short on money so it came in handy. However, the next morning, I was so stiff and sore that I could hardly move; and I spent most of the day in my hotel room in bed, missing the trip to the Statute of Liberty.

In 1958 one only needed to be eighteen in order to buy alcoholic drinks in New York. I was seventeen at the time. We knew that if we got caught drinking alcohol that we would be sent home so I waited until the last night of our stay in New York City. At about seven in the evening, when I thought the coast-was-clear, I walked across the street into a bar. I sat on a bar stool and ordered a glass of beer. I didn't have any fake identification so if they asked for an ID, I would have just left abruptly. The bartender served me and I sat there listening to a couple have some sort of a heated discussion.

The woman turned to me, as I recall, and said, "Do you know anything about painting?"

I recalled to myself how I had painted my uncle's fence and house so I had responded, "Yah, I know something about painting."

"So okay mister expert, was it Van Gogh or Monet who painted

Irises?"

I was in mild shock since I quickly realized that they were arguing about art, not painting a house. My dad used to say once in a while, "It's better to remain silent and be thought a fool, than open your mouth and remove all doubt." In spite of that I forged ahead, "I think it was Monet," I said.

Apparently, I had agreed with him and his girlfriend shot me a nasty look. I later found out that the correct answer was Van Gogh.

I had three glasses of beer and was feeling a warm glow spread throughout my body when I realized that I had better go back to the hotel. Then, and only then, did I began to worry about a chaperone seeing me go into or leaving the bar; or someone smelling beer on my breath. I walked quickly out of the bar, took a left, walked about a block, and then crossed the street. As I approached the front of the hotel, I could see a couple of the chaperones talking in the lobby. I thought, *Did they see me? Were they going to confront me when I walk in?*

I remember deciding that I had done a stupid thing, and I would confess it all to them if they asked, even the story about the painting. I walked into the hotel, both chaperones greeted me from about twenty feet, and I said hello and headed for the elevator. Waiting for the elevator, I expected a hand on my shoulder at any second. When the elevator opened, I quickly got in and pushed the "close door" and then punched the floor of my room. My roommate Jerry Johnson doubted my story until I let him smell my breath.

The next day we left for home and I was completely broke. I borrowed money from my friend Bob Radloff to get a sandwich out of a vending machine before we left for Grand Central Station and the ride back to Minnesota. Two weeks in Washington D.C. and New York City were unforgettable experiences for a Midwestern kid of seventeen and well worth the 200 dollars that I had borrowed for the trip.

Senior Skip Day

On senior skip day, some of us headed out to Todd Park, a beautiful park of about one hundred twenty-seven acres on the very north side of Austin. The park had recreational areas for both children and adults. There were many public restrooms, a number of shelter areas with picnic tables, and limestone fireplaces for cooking. A small creek also meandered through the park helping to nourish the appetites of the massive oak and elm trees located everywhere, but not on the ball diamonds. Some of the senior class girls made arrangements for a huge picnic with hamburgers, baked beans, potato chips and potato salad, cakes and cookies, and all kinds of soft drinks.

Bob Radloff was one of my classmates, and the only one who had a brand new Mercury convertible. Bob lived on a farm southwest of Austin and had sold some of his livestock to purchase the car. The girls needed some more ice and I asked Bob if I could borrow his car to run into town and get the ice. He agreed, but warned me about staying away from the high school. I told him that I would stay away from the high school and left for town.

Austin High School is a beautiful old three-story brick Gothic styled building, which is approximately two blocks long and one block wide. On the west side of the high school at that time was the vocational school, which could be reached by going through an underground tunnel. Kenwood Avenue ran between the high school and the vocational school. Because of the structure of the two buildings, the avenue provided a magnified sound of vehicles driving by.

Bob had two Hollywood mufflers on his Mercury that had a gentle purr to them when driven normally. The temptation on that spring skip day was overwhelming, and I put the Merc in low gear and pushed the speed of the car up to about forty miles per hour until I got

66

between the two buildings. Then I just backed off the accelerator and the mufflers howled, cracked, snapped, and popped as I knew they would through the open high school windows. I just knew good ol' Bob would understand.

When I got back to the park everybody was ready to eat, and I shared my driving episode with some of the guys and girls. After lunch some of us got into a softball game and others just sat around and talked. When the ball game was done, I heard a big commotion down by the river and a bunch of the guys were throwing each other into the muddy stream. I had no desire to get involved in that mud-slinging atmosphere so I stayed a fair distance away. One of the guys involved in the river activity was my good friend Jim Baldwin and he had a clean old Plymouth car.

Jim Baldwin came up to me and asked me if I would drive his car since I was still clean and dry. He would also have two other guys who would be riding in the back seat. I agreed to do that. When we got over by his car, Jim took off all of his clothes and told the other two guys to do the same if they wanted a ride home. He didn't want them sitting on his car seats with their wet and muddy clothes. They reluctantly agreed.

I was driving down Main Street at a busy time of the day and Jim reached over and started blowing the horn. The noise, of course, caused people to look in our direction and that's the first I knew that the two guys in the back seat had their bare butts nearly hanging out the back windows. It was not "Moon over Miami," but they were "mooning" Austin shoppers. What could I do but laugh and yell as Jim continued to blow the horn. Shortly after I turned east off of main street, I was pulled over by "Austin's Finest." Wouldn't you know, as we cruised Main, there would be a policeman in a car. I pulled the car over and everybody sat down. I was at a loss for words when the officer asked me just what were we trying to do?

"Just on our way home from senior skip day, Cliff. They got wet and Jim didn't want his upholstery ruined."

We had lucked out that the officer was one of my neighbors. Cliff sternly said, "Get those guys home and keep their bare asses on the seats until you get there or things are gonna happen."

"Yes, sir, Cliff. Thanks and we're out of here." By the time he got back into his squad car, we were already a block away. Wild Jim was still hooting as I drove out of the downtown business area of town.

Working and Two Tries at College

My first year out of high school, I tried to go to Austin Community College and work from 10 p.m. to 6 a.m. in a local gas station. Although the gas-pumping business was slow during those work hours, I also was required to "detail" one car per shift. Detailing one car per night meant that I vacuumed and shampooed the interior, steam-cleaned the engine compartment, and polished and buffed the exterior of the car. I believe that the owner got fifty dollars for each of the cars done from a local car dealer, and my gross wages for the eight-hour shift were probably about fifteen dollars. You can see with the mathematics why he wanted one car done per night.

Going to college in the day time at the community college and working at night left me no time for a social life or for studying. I was doomed for failure. My brother David had recently been discharged from the navy, and he was attending the community college too. One day I told him that I just didn't have time to study for a test in algebra class and David said, "No sweat, algebra's easy for me. Just sit behind me and I'll give you the answers to the questions. You can create phony work to make the instructor believe you have the right answer." Although I knew that cheating was wrong, I thought at the time that it was a better alternative than failing.

I sat behind Brother Dave for the algebra exam. Everything was working perfectly as he slipped me back his answers to the questions, and the instructor hadn't noticed anything. Two days later, I was sitting in the class and anxiously awaiting the results of our recent test. The instructor, a nerd-before-his-time with high-water pants and white socks was explaining the "Bell Curve" to the class, and I thought, *Give me a break, Nerdy, give us the test results back.*

David had a perfect paper. I had a zero. It seems that Dr. Nerd had handed out different tests to every other person. Doom. I dropped out of college shortly thereafter. So I had quit going to the community college, and my fiancée, who was going to Butler University in Indiana, was upset with me for being a college dropout. Money was not an issue for her.

Work Gloves and Plumbing

After I quit going to the community college in 1958, I wasn't having much luck finding a job and my dad said to me, "Go out to Schied Plumbing and Heating; I heard he has a job available. Also, put a pair of work gloves in your back pocket in case he wants you to go right to work." Putting work gloves in my back pocket when going to a job interview was beyond my comprehension, and I felt my dad was not with the times. I did it anyway.

The next day I went out to Schied Plumbing & Heating to apply for a job. I walked into the office and announced who I was and asked the receptionist for a job application. I filled it out and brought it back up to the counter. The receptionist said that there were no openings, but she would file my application. I asked for an interview with Mr. Schied, and she told me that he was too busy and repeated that there weren't any jobs available.

Mr. Schied, who was sitting in his office and I'm certain could hear our conversation, interrupted our conversation and invited me into his office. I had never met him before and found that he was a very pleasant man. He complimented me about my athletic career (he had a son Larry who was a junior in high school and a very good athlete at Pacelli High School in Austin). Mr. Schied wanted to know what my future plans were. I told him that I had dropped out of the community college and that I wanted to earn enough money so that I could go to college successfully.

Mr. Schied told me on that Friday that I should report to work on the following Monday and that I would be commuting out of town with his brother Bill. I thanked Mr. Schied for his time; and over the course of the next few years, I was occasionally humiliated by my father when he would relate how I had been hired by Emil Schied because I had work gloves in my back pocket. That may have been the reason, but I think it was probably out of the goodness of Mr. Schied's heart that he hired me.

Emil Schied was also the manager of the Austin Packer's Baseball Team. In the fifties in southern Minnesota, that team was the team to beat and was the equivalent of Triple AAA professional clubs today. There were many games during that era when there were in excess of five-thousand fans at those ball games. Sometimes Emil used to suck on a lemon as he stood in the third-base coaching box. Fans had an easy way to give him verbal response about the ball players, the lemon, or their feelings toward him.

There seemed to be a lot more verbal abuse then there is now by fans. Maybe it was because we were a lot closer to the field and fans knew that what they yelled would be heard by the manager or ball players. A number of players from Mr. Schied's teams ended up in the major leagues, most notably Bill "Moose" Skowron, who played a number of years for the New York Yankees.

There was always the scuttle-butt from other Southern Minnesota teams that either the Hormel plant or Emil Schied had hired outstanding players from out of state to play for the Austin Packers. If that was true, was there something wrong with that?

I worked for Schied Plumbing & Heating for nearly a year in Northfield, Minnesota. In the course of that year, we put an addition on a private elementary school and an addition on the local hospital.

When we were working on the addition to the elementary school, I had the job of pounding through a one-foot poured concrete wall with a three-pound hammer and a steel point. The point was shaped like a tent-stake, and I started out chipping cement by hand with a circle of approximately three feet. This was not my idea, but the foreman's, Bill Schied. I knew nothing about pounding through cement walls. I learned in a hurry and it was an exceedingly slow process trying to pound my way through a cement wall. The eventual hole would need to be approximately sixteen inches in diameter to be able to accommodate a twelve-inch steam line coming from the boiler on the other side of the wall of the old building.

I don't remember how many days it took me to pound through that wall. I do remember that every so often, I would have one of the steamfitters regrind my dull steel point. I also remember that approximately every five hundred times that I hit that steel point trying to drive through that concrete wall that the hammer would glance off of that steel point and hit me on the left hand. I would yell and curse a blue streak and throw the hammer against the wall. I remember that I broke three hammer handles that way. I also remember that I had a permanent bruise on my left hand for two months after I had broken through that cement wall. I had decided at that time that I did not want to be a construction laborer for my life's work.

I had a good working relationship with all of the workers on the job in Northfield, so much so that they would warn me when the local union labor business agent was on the site. Initially, I had not joined the union because nobody had asked me to join. It became a game then with the union members of the plumbers, steamfitters, etcetera. that when the business labor agent came on the property for the labor union they would warn me. They would say, "Junior, hit the tunnels; here comes the business agent." And, I would hide below in the four-foot by four-foot tunnels where we were building the water, heating, and sewer lines. I guess because of my age I had become the job-site "junior." This whole game was amusing to all of the job-site workers except the union labor business manager. One day he came on the job and announced, "If you don't produce that "labor scab, I'm going to shut this job down!"

The game-playing was over and my union-working friends called me up from the tunnel below. I joined the labor brotherhood that day, but attended only one meeting before I was convinced that the whole thing was a scam. I had run better meetings and had required more accountability as a high school student council president than were required at that meeting of the brotherhood.

There were times when I assisted a couple of the steamfitters in the tunnels of the elementary school where I wondered if it was reality. Each of them had a half-pint of blackberry brandy for the morning and another for the afternoon to get them though the day. Their welding work was fine, but their breath was gross. I stayed in Northfield, at the Jesse James Hotel, for two weeks because of bad driving conditions in the winter. It seemed like the better choice rather than driving back and forth with "Wild-Bill Schied" in his '49 Ford with holes in the floorboards in the freezing Minnesota winter.

During my two-week stay in Northfield, the two steamfitters would take me downtown to the municipal liquor store in Northfield and we would have some drinks at 4 p.m. I was nineteen and they were in their late thirties or early forties. By 6 p.m. I was high, had gone to have something to eat, and was back sleeping in the hotel. I think that they closed up the bar every night.

When we were putting the addition on the Northfield Hospital, I had an interesting experience. One day in the winter of 1959, I walked over to a window of the existing hospital and discovered that there was the operating room and that an operation was taking place at that time. I had never seen an operating room nor had been in an operating room. They were amputating someone's foot. I was flabbergasted that they looked like they were using a common hacksaw in a hospital. I had never thought about what kind of tools or instruments might be used in an amputation.

I left work for Shied Plumbing & Heating Company in Austin and had an athletic football scholarship at South Dakota State College in Brookings, South Dakota in 1959. I was a starting half back on offense and a defensive back on defense. At that time, freshmen were not eligible to play on the varsity.

The last game of the football season for us was in Fargo with North Dakota State University. We ended up winning the game, which was played in a snow storm. Near the end of the game, we were on their ten-yard line and my play was called. When I got tackled, I felt a pain in my shoulder and I went over to the side line and told the coach. He gave me the same play and sent me back into the game. I got to the one-yard line before I got tackled again. The pain in my shoulder was immense, as I recall. I was taken out of the game and we scored on the next play.

In the locker room after the game, they had to cut my jersey off and help me remove my equipment. I tried to take a shower, but the pain was too great. I told the coach that I thought I should go to the hospital for x-rays, but he said he thought it was just a bruise. I knew better, and I was beginning to think that they were more concerned about the expense of possibly leaving me at the hospital in Fargo than they were about my injury. My friends helped me get dressed. I was somewhat embarrassed by the whole ordeal, and it was the first time that I had been injured in college football.

The bus ride back to our campus was over two hundred miles and I was miserable the whole way. My shoulder seemed to be the shock-absorber for the bus on every bump. We stopped to eat and some of my teammates cut up my food for me. When we got back to Brookings, South Dakota, they took me to the hospital for x-rays.

The x-rays showed that I had a broken clavicle or "collarbone" in layman's terms. They decided to keep me overnight for observation. When the attractive young nurse got me to my room, she asked me if I needed help getting undressed. Although I was nineteen, there was no way that I was going to let a nurse undress me. The doctor in the emergency room had placed my arm in a sling and had given me a pain pill. There was no way to place a cast on a broken collarbone. So I had on a hospital gown with the ties in the back, wash pants, underwear, shoes, and socks.

The nurse told me to leave my clothes on the chair by the bed and she would come back and hang them up in the closet. There was an old man in the room as well and he seemed to be amused by what he was seeing. I took off my clothes and climbed up into the bed. I was amazed at how much of my body seemed to be connected to that broken bone and how uncomfortable every move I made was to that area of my body. I could tell that I wasn't going to be a model patient.

About fifteen minutes later, the young nurse came back into the room and was putting my clothes in the closet. She inquired of me,

"Didn't you have any underwear?"

"Sure I do."

"Well, where is it?"

"I'm wearing my underwear."

"You can't wear your underwear in this hospital."

"The heck I can't," I replied.

"Well, we'll see about that," she said, as she stormed out of the room.

The old man in the other bed was giggling through the whole conversation. Then the old man said, "Why don't you let her take your underwear off; it might be kind of fun." And he giggled again.

For lack of a better thing to say I responded back to the old goat,

"Sir, it's the principle of the thing." *College had taught me something,* I confided to myself.

As I lay on that bed, I tried to think of what kind of options I had.

I really couldn't think of any options, other than leaving. Besides, it was now close to 1 a.m. and I was tired after a long day including a long bus ride to Fargo, playing a football game in a snow storm, and the long ride back

Then I heard the young nurse talking to a supervisor out in the hall and telling the supervisor the great dilemma of this football player who would not pass his shorts to her. Although they were talking softly, I could still hear them. The supervisor told the young nurse to wait until I went to sleep and then go in and take the shorts from me. There existed, at that time, a hospital philosophy that underwear was some how totally detrimental to the healing process.

The sly young nurse came in and asked me how I was doing and said, "Have a good night's sleep." I stayed awake listening to the ol' man snore until after 2 a.m. That young nurse came back twice; I presume looking for my underwear. I figured I had won that contest. I thought it was a pretty stupid rule. The next morning when I awoke I was being brought breakfast. I was starved. When I sat up to eat was the first that I noticed that my shorts were gone. What a surprise. What a surprise. The old man in the other bed just looked at me and gave me a big toothless smile.

I left South Dakota State College at Christmas break and did not return. At nineteen years old, I had already dropped out of college twice. I wasn't certain what I would do.

The Nineteen Sixties

Volunteering for the Draft

When I left college at winter break in 1959, I went home and volunteered for the draft in the U.S. Army. College was not going well. I was struggling with an engagement to a hometown sweetheart who was going to college in Indiana, and I was still healing from a football injury. Volunteering for the draft seemed like the only thing to do at the time. I needed to mature and get my career goals straightened out.

The local draft quota was full for December and January, 1960. By February, I was pretty well-healed from my football injury so I went out to South Dakota to try and mend my ways and get my athletic scholarship restored. They agreed to restore my scholarship, and I drove back to Austin elated that everything had worked out. The following Monday, the local draft board in Mower County, Minnesota informed me that they had drafted me into the army the previous week and that I would be inducted in March, 1960, for two years.

Induction and Army Training

I reported to Minneapolis, was given a very basic physical, was sworn in and left by bus for processing at Fort Carson, Colorado. After a few days of tests, uniform issue, haircuts, and general harassment, we boarded a plane (my first air trip) for Fort Benning, Georgia, and the infantry. It was March, 1960.

In my hometown, there were less than ten black people out of a population of approximately 22,000. If the truth were known in that town, in my opinion, it would have shown that there indeed were bias and prejudice towards all minority races and ethnic groups. The people living there thought that they were Christians and very accepting of all ethnic groups and races. I had been brought up and educated in the schools and churches in that culture. College had exposed me to some diversity, but had not prepared me for what I would witness in the South.

When we exited the military plane from Colorado to Fort Benning, Georgia, I was shocked to see separate drinking fountains and restrooms labeled "colored." Even though I had good friends who were black in the army, we could not ride in the same car off the post in Columbus, Georgia, or we would be arrested. It was a rude awakening for a small-town boy from southern Minnesota.

The black soldiers who seemed to have the biggest trouble adjusting, however, were the army men who had come from the northern part of the United States. Freedoms that they had experienced at home were gone in the South. I could understand and empathize with their bitterness.

I had been drafted into a special experimental unit of the infantry at Fort Benning. We were together for two years and we went through basic infantry training, advanced infantry training, basic unit training, and advanced unit training for a total of eight months training. The rationale given to us for all of our training and the reason that we would be together for two years was that personnel in the Korean conflict and World War II did not necessarily know their "fighting partners," those who were with them in combat. There was no question that we got to know each other over the course of the two years.

We had a break and were able to take leave after the first sixteen weeks of training and after thirty-two weeks of training. Before I left for basic training, I had broken my engagement with Aneitta, my fiancée who had left Butler University in Indianapolis and returned back to Austin. We just had too many differences. One of my buddies from Austin, Dick "Smiley" Gaughran sent me a news-clipping in Georgia when Aneitta married another high school classmate, a few months later.

One of my friends in infantry training in Georgia was a guy named Clyde Ebbs from Colorado. Ebbs was a no-nonsense cowboy who stood about six-foot-five inches tall. With me at five-foot-ten, Ebbs and I probably looked like the old comic strip characters of Mutt and Jeff. Clyde did have a good sense of humor and we had many good times together in Georgia and some in Korea.

Near the middle of our training at Fort Benning, Georgia, we got a fresh graduate from the Officer Candidate School, OCS, which we called the ninety-day wonders (OCS training lasted for three months). There were three kinds of officers in the army: those from Officers Candidate School, those from the ROTC (Reserve Officer Training Corp) who were college graduates, and those from West Point. Most of us in the army enlisted rank thought that the officers from ROTC were the best and most humane, followed by OCS, and lastly the "dudes" from West Point. West Pointers always seemed arrogant and too much concerned with discipline and rules.

As I was beginning to say, we had a new platoon leader who had just graduated from OCS. His name was Lieutenant Brito. At the end of his first week with us, he came into our platoon for an inspection. The place was immaculate. The floor was polished, all bunks neat and tidy, foot lockers and wall lockers open and spotless. "Lieutenant Jerk" came in and started tearing up bunks and tipping over foot lockers. I guess he wanted to make a tough first impression.

We were all standing at attention by our foot lockers when he was making an ass of himself in front of "veteran" infantrymen. He asked many stupid questions as he walked around the platoon bay with a sergeant-first-class (SFC) following him around, but occasionally making a funny face behind "Lieutenant Jerk." We secretly called the SFC "Sergeant Bilko" as seen in a television series at that time, with the same name starring Phil Silvers during the sixties.

When five-foot-six "Lieutenant Fuzz" got over to Private Clyde Ebbs, the six-foot-five Colorado cowboy, he said, "Hi, Ebbs, how ya doing?"

"Just fine, sir."

"How's your collar brass, Ebbs? You're too tall; I can't see it."

"Just fine sir."

Lieutenant Brito said, "How's the weather up there, Ebbs?"

Ebbs replied after watching Brito tip over his buddy's footlocker, "Just fine, sir, how's the weather down around my ass?"

The whole platoon broke up in laughter.

"Lieutenant Fuzz" was so infuriated that he, an officer of the United States Army, had been treated like that and he stormed out of the platoon saying, "You're going to jail, Ebbs; you're going to jail!"

We heard later that day from one of our buddies who was a clerk in the company commander's office that when "Lieutenant Fuzz" had told Captain Stallings, our company commander, of his encounter with Ebbs, that the company commander had just roared with laughter. Ebbs grew in stature that day, and Lieutenant Brito learned an important lesson about human relation skills.

When we went on leave prior to our departure as a unit for Korea in February, 1961, Lieutenant Brito lectured our platoon about not getting married when we were home because we would be gone for a year in Korea. I don't recall if any of my buddies got married when they were on that two-week leave prior to our departure, but I do recall Lieutenant Brito's new wife sending him off as we embarked on our journey and a whole lot of us giving him cat-calls as he and his new wife embraced.

My next military year was spent in Camp Kaiser, South Korea, just south of the demilitarized zone, DMZ, separating North and South Korea.

Camp Kaiser, Korea 1961-1962

Camp Kaiser, Korea is located just south of the demilitarized zone that exists between the northern border of South Korea and the southern border of North Korea. As I recall Seoul, Korea, was a couple hours drive south of Camp Kaiser or approximately fifty miles. We were lucky if we could average thirty-five miles an hour driving military vehicles through the mountains and marginal roads.

Shortly after we arrived at Camp Kaiser, Korea, we became members of the famed 7th Infantry Division (known as the hourglass division because the round insignia looked like a black hour glass on a red background). I competed with several other men from other infantry platoons from our battle group to be Colonel Patterson's personal radio operator, when we were out training in the field. I was selected so I was moved up to Headquarters' Company and became a part of the radio communication team. My job dealt strictly with voice communications since I had not been trained in other methods, such as the Morse code. When we were out in the field training, I was always with the colonel and operated his radio communications with the other five infantry companies.

When at our post compound in Camp Kaiser, I lived in a Quonset hut with nine other soldiers. The hut was made of steel, with virtually no insulation. In the winter time, the weather was similar to the weather in Minnesota, so we kept the two kerosene stoves burning red hot to keep us warm. In the winter by early morning, the stoves always ran out of fuel and then the bickering would begin. The bickering was about whose turn it was to get up in the cold building, get dressed, and get more fuel for the two stoves. As I look back at it, I did more than my share of getting the fuel since it seemed to be easier than lying around and bickering about the cold.

When we weren't pulling our six-hour shift on the radio, we played cards, read, played table tennis, or played billiards in our company area.

There was an enlisted men's club about one hundred feet away from us and sometimes we went up there for happy hour. You can't imagine how drunk and sick guys got for less than a dollar. During happy hour, you could get a shot of whiskey with a beer wash for ten cents. At the PX (Post Exchange), you could buy a carton of cigarettes for a dollar and ten cents. Some of the guys, in their mid-twenties in my Quonset, were so irresponsible that I would collect five dollars and fifty cents from them every pay day and buy them their cigarettes for the month.

I had made the rank of Specialist IV in a little over a year, a pay grade of E-4, and that meant with "over-seas pay" that I got paid one hundred fifty dollars per month. The mess hall didn't have very good food so we spent a lot of our money at the PX buying cheeseburgers, fries, and sodas. A short distance away, one could get a shampoo, hair cut, shave, and a head and neck massage for seventy-five cents.

We had a "house-boy," who was really an adult Korean man who was married and had a family. He made our bunks every day, cleaned our Quonset, shined our shoes, and did our laundry for each of us for a gross total of forty-five dollars per month. Were we spoiled or what? It made living in that crummy place a little easier to handle.

The infantry companies spent nearly half of their time training out in the field. We at Headquarters Company seldom went with them, but we always kept radio communications with them when they were out training.

Colonel Patterson, our Battle Group Commander, was kind of soft when it came to living out doors. When we went out in the field for training, he lived in a home-made camping trailer. One time when we were out in the field, he needed some shaving lotion so he sent his driver and me back to Camp Kaiser to get some for him. His combat steel pot for his helmet was in the jeep so I put it on when we got on the road. We ran into several marchers and other vehicles; and when they saw the eagle on my helmet, they would render me a salute. I would just touch my brow with my hand in a mock-salute and wave to them. You can imagine that many of those guys who saluted me must have thought that at twenty years old I didn't look like a full-bird colonel. The driver got nervous as we approached Camp Kaiser so I took the steel pot off and placed it back on the seat. It was fun being "Colonel Johnson" for a brief time.

Good Conduct Award

In March of 1962, I was presented the Good Conduct Award by the battle group commander. I was told that it was unusual at that time to get this award for less than two years of service. Shortly thereafter was the last time that I came in contact with the colonel and it was not pleasant.

Frequently, when we went through the pay line, we were asked to contribute to some charitable cause. Most of the time, I as well as others did contribute. On that last pay day in March, 1962, we were told that the division commander wanted a one hundred percent donation to the American Red Cross. I didn't give. When I didn't give to the cause, the captain in charge of payroll said that I would probably be called in by my company commander, who also had the rank of captain.

We had less than a month of duty remaining in Korea and our tour of duty had been extended two months because of the Cuban Missile Crisis, so we were anxious to go home. After another seventeen-day ship ride across the Pacific Ocean, I would be discharged in Oakland, California.

My last couple of weeks in Korea, I had the 2 a.m. to 8 a.m. shift on the radio communications network. It was pretty soft duty. Get off work, sleep until about 4 p.m. and then I had the time to myself until 2 a.m. the next morning. I had gone four days without shaving because I seldom saw any officers. It was a game and my buddies were enjoying it as much as I was. At the time my beard was pretty dark, even though my hair was blonde, and I have a picture that a buddy took as evidence.

On the fifth day of my non-shaving, my platoon sergeant relieved me on the radio and told me to go directly to the company commander's office at 7:30 a.m. I thought my goose was cooked and I was reporting there because of my beard. What kind of discipline that I would receive I was not certain.

I reported to the company commander in my wrinkled fatigues, unshaven, and a little nervous. He said nothing of my appearance but questioned why I had not given to the Red Cross on the last payday. I remember telling him that it was based upon principle. The only thing that I saw the Red Cross doing in Korea was coming once a week to our camp, and we had mandatory attendance to go for coffee, donuts, and silly games with young attractive Red Cross workers dressed in imitation army fatigues. The company commander said that I would have to see the "ol' man" if I didn't give. I told him that would be fine, and I was dismissed. I went back to my hooch, got my shaving kit, went up to the latrine, and shaved.

The next day I was told to report to the Sergeant Major at battle group headquarters. There were very few Sergeant Majors in the army and they carried a lot weight. If you had a weak colonel in charge of a battle group, as many thought of our commander, the Sergeant-Major more or less was running the battle group. A Sergeant Major is the highest rank for non-commissioned officers in the army.

I reported to the Sergeant Major (he had been the one who had recommended me over several other candidates to run the colonel's radios). I liked and respected him. I did not waver, however, when he asked me to donate to the Red Cross. When I said no, he suggested that he would donate a dollar on my behalf and I said no to his offer as well. We parted by his statement that I would probably have to see the "ol' man" about not giving to the Red Cross. I said that would be fine.

Two days later, my platoon leader told me to report directly to Colonel Patterson at his office. I was met there by the Sergeant Major who had me sit in a chair and wait for approximately thirty minutes. I supposed this was to raise my level of anxiety, and it worked a little bit. What the wait did for me was to stiffen my resolve to not give in to the Red Cross donation.

When the Sergeant Major said that I could go into the battle group commander's office, I complied. Upon entering the Colonel's office, I came to attention, rendered a hand salute, and was not put at ease. After the colonel returned my salute, he moved to within about one-foot of me and kept me at attention during our very brief exchange, which went something like this:

The colonel said, "How are you doing today, Johnson?"

"Just fine sir." He smelled like garlic, onions, and stale booze.

"I understand that you are scheduled to go home next month, Johnson."

"Yes, sir."

"You do want to go home as scheduled, don't you, Johnson?"

"Yes, sir. Have the plans changed, sir?"

"Sometimes, I wonder why I gave you that Good Conduct Award. Um, I understand that you have not given to the division commander's request for one hundred percent contributing to the Red Cross."

"That's correct, sir, and I don't plan to give." As I spoke, I thought, *Didn't this guy brush his teeth.*

"Well the ol' man wants one hundred percent and we surely don't want a black eye coming from this battle group, do we Johnson? We've worked together for over a year, and I'm surprised at your decision. How about if I donate a couple of bucks to this effort on your behalf?"

I was becoming concerned that just maybe this guy had enough clout to keep me from going home on time and I was tired of Korea. I wasn't about to volunteer giving up my Good Conduct Medal. "Well, sir, you do what you have to do, but I'm not giving to the Red Cross."

Colonel turning away from me, "Sergeant Major, escort this soldier out of my office."

I left Colonel Patterson's office without saluting him. I never saw him again before I left on schedule for the United States about a month later and I received an honorable discharge.

The Suggestion Contest

Shortly before I left Korea in the spring of 1962, an order came down from the commanding general of the 7th Infantry Division that each person under his command would offer a suggestion to improve the operations of the division. As any army veteran knows when an order comes down, it goes through the chain-of-command and eventually reached us through our platoon sergeant. They didn't care what we suggested, but it had to be in writing and given to the platoon sergeant. Some of my buddies were kind of silly and they suggested having beer in the drinking fountains, twenty-hour work weeks, and the like. I decided I would submit a serious suggestion.

When we walked about two hundred feet south from our Quonset hut, in Korea known as hooch, we were at a cement block building known as our mess hall. This was the place where the army provided us our meals. About another one hundred feet south of the mess hall and up the hill to the southwest was our latrine. For some unknown reason, there was a sewer-gas release through a pipe coming down from the latrine that rose approximately six feet above the ground and was located about fifty feet west of our mess hall. When we stood in line waiting for our "chow" if the wind was out of the west or southwest, the stench from that sewer-gas release pipe was too much. Many times it ruined our appetites, and we just walked away from the chow line. We had complained about the odor the whole year that we had been there, but nothing had happened to change the situation.

What I did was take a sheet of blank paper and laid out a basic picture of the problem with a very simple solution to the problem; move that sewer-gas release pipe from its existing location. That was my suggestion to the commanding general of the 7th Infantry Division for his "Suggestion Contest."

Approximately two months later after an honorable discharge and residing in Austin, Minnesota, I got a letter from the headquarters of the 7th Infantry Division in Korea. Enclosed in the envelope was a letter of commendation, a check for twenty-five dollars, and a certificate acknowledging that I had won second place in the 7th Infantry Division Suggestion Contest. I was somewhat flabbergasted, and I always wondered what suggestion had won first place. I spent the money, but I still have the framed second-place certificate hanging next to other army memorabilia.

The Lost Term Paper

After graduating from Austin Community College in 1964, I was a junior at Mankato State University in Mankato, Minnesota (known today as Minnesota State University at Mankato). I worked as a bartender between twenty and twenty-five hours per week for approximately one dollar and seventy-five cents per hour at Michael's Restaurant in Mankato. Michael's was owned by the Pappas bothers in Rochester, Minnesota, and was a classy place with good food and spirits. During my junior year in college, I also began to receive educational benefits through a new federally legislated G.I. Bill. That amounted to about one hundred fifty dollars per month, which essentially paid for my books and tuition. My wife worked too, and I made no student loans during any of my college education years spanning the next four decades.

I had a term paper due for one of my education psychology classes. I had taught myself how to type while working the night shift as a radio operator in Korea. I had some months earlier gone to an auction in Mankato and purchased an old relic-of-a-typewriter for five bucks. The keys on that manual typewriter needed to be stroked really hard and that was okay because I typed really slowly. As I recall, I had done considerable research and had discussed some of the behaviors associated with gangs in New York for that particular paper. The paper was probably about ten pages long including the bibliography. Of course, I used carbon paper so that I would have a copy of the final product. My copy had lots of smudges on it from the carbon paper due to corrections that I had made on the original.

I had labored away at that old mechanical typewriter to complete that term paper about gangs in New York. On the day of the class that the paper was due, I drove over to the upper campus of the university in my old beat-up '53 Ford, found a parking space, grabbed the term paper and my notebook, and headed for a student lounge just down the hall from my psych class. I got a lousy cup of coffee out of a vending machine and lit up a Pall Mall. Smoking had become a bad habit when I was in the army in Korea. I was never smart enough to smoke filtered cigarettes, I had tried them but they just didn't taste as good. There were always some students from the psych class in the lounge, and we'd make small talk for about fifteen minutes before the class began.

When the appointed time came, we went to class. That particular educational psychology teacher would spend up to half the course period lamenting on how he was ostracized by the rest of the male members of his department. As I recall his name was Cansler or something like that. For the first few weeks of the class, I thought he was setting us up to demonstrate some psychological theorem or behavior demonstration with his ranting about his psychology teaching peers. I was wrong. I believed then that he was just plain paranoid or maybe just plain nuts. That particular day he began by asking us to pass in our term papers. I looked down at my desk and there was no term paper, there was no notebook, there was nothing. I looked quickly at the guys sitting next to me to see if they had my materials. I was twenty-four years old. It was not a time for fun and games. They didn't have my materials. I told the assistant professor that I must have left my materials in the lounge, and he gave me one of those "Oh, you haven't written the paper, have you?" looks.

I walked briskly back to the lounge and found nothing but empty coffee containers and ash trays with snuffed-out cigarettes. I stood and mentally tried to recount my steps. I remembered that when I had left the car, I had my notebook and the term paper with me. I remembered having it on the table in the student lounge as I had my coffee and cigarette. Then I recalled I went to class. So where was the term paper?

I went back to class and interrupted Assistant Professor Cansler, not-as-yet-tenured, talking about his department chair. I told him that I couldn't find my notebook or the term paper, and someone must have stolen them. He gave me one of those "You're a liar, Nathan" looks; although, I'm certain he had no idea what my name was in a class of about fifteen students.

I told him, "I have a carbon copy at home and I'll go get it right now."

He responded, "That's okay, if it doesn't show up bring your copy to the next class." I have no idea what happened in the rest of the class that day because I was preoccupied with trying to determine where I had left my term paper or who had stolen my term paper.

Two days had passed since I had lost my term paper and on Friday I was back over in the university lounge, having a lousy cup of coffee and cig, and prepared to take my carbon-copy term paper into the psych class. There was a custodian picking up some garbage, and I asked him if he had found a term paper and a notebook and he had not.

I decided to stop at the men's room before I went to class and there on a shelf above the urinal were my notebook and term paper. I had forgotten one of Nathan's footprints on the previous Wednesday, a brief trip to the restroom.

Selling Basketball Tickets

One time as a teacher at Waterville-Elysian High School, I needed to get some petty cash. I needed a small amount of cash and a cash box because I was going to sell some athletic game tickets. I went down to the Superintendent John Kunelius' office.

As part of the Superintendent's Office, at that time, there was a huge walk-in vault that had a door about ten inches thick, as you'd typically see in a bank. I figured with all of that armor, it would take a tank to get inside that vault, if it were locked.

Although I saw and frequently talked with the superintendent, I hadn't been in his office since I had interviewed for the job several months earlier. As I entered his office, I told him why I was there, and he got up from behind his desk to assist me. I assumed the money would be in the vault so I turned around and walked into the vault. Imagine my surprise when I looked around in the vault and saw new footballs, basketballs, volleyballs, and the like. What a surprise! What a surprise!

The superintendent had walked past the open vault door out to the adjacent business office and stopped at the counter. He was standing by the counter with a big grin on his face as I came out of the vault. He then reached down under the counter and produced the cash box for my event. The importance he placed on cash and athletic equipment was indelibly marked in my mind.

Cigar Smoke

The first year that I taught at Waterville-Elysian High School was in 1966, and I commuted from Mankato, Minnesota, a distance of approximately twenty-five miles one way.

Sometimes I drove to school by myself, and sometimes with one, two, or three other teachers in a car pool. Most of the time, my car pool consisted of just Loren Ringham, a guy who taught in the elementary school and me. He was a cigar smoker and that even bothered me as a cigarette smoker, especially when we were in such a confined space.

We would alternate driving the twenty-five miles from Mankato to Waterville every other week. I had a less than one-year-old 1965 Mustang, my first nice car. Loren would light up a cigar on the way over on the ride to school, gently snuff it out when we arrived at the school, and leave it in the ashtray. Then later that day when we left for home, he'd light up that old "stogie" and puff on it until we got to Mankato.

He told me that his wife didn't know that he smoked, and I thought surely that the cigar smoke must have affected his ability to reason. You could smell cigar smoke when you were ten feet away from him.

About the time that I got that wretched cigar-smoke smell out of my car, it was my turn to drive again. That stinking cigar smoke was one of the things that convinced me to move to Waterville and rent a small house my second year of teaching.

Snow Days and Garbage Trucks

Most rural public schools and some urban school districts in Minnesota build snow days into their calendars. Typically, a school district would add a few days beyond the state-mandated number of annual school days for snow days. That way, when blizzards occurred, and most winters had at least one during the school year, the administration made early morning announcements over the radio and television stations that school would not be in session that day. Most students and teachers liked those unpredicted mini-vacations. Most parents didn't.

The first year that I taught in 1966, I commuted about twenty-five miles one-way, each day. Sometimes in the winters, as commuters, we were on the road to work when we would hear that school had been closed that day.

One particular storm began on a Saturday and raged day and night for three days. Nearly everything was closed in the state including all retail stores and other businesses. The governor closed all of the schools in Minnesota not only because of the horrendous road conditions, but also because of the life-threatening wind chills.

That snowy day in 1967, the snow was so deep in my driveway that I couldn't even open the garage door. If I would have shoveled out the driveway, it would have been blown full in a matter of hours anyway. My 1965 Mustang was too low for that deep snow. Although I loved that old Ford, it was also powered by the rear wheels and there was very little weight over the back tires. So even if I could have gotten out of the garage, I would not have been able to drive very far without

96

getting stuck.

By Monday I was pacing the floor and I needed to get out of the house. I called Dutch Lyons, a self-proclaimed sanitary engineer. Dutch was a character, and he had a contract with the city of Mankato to pick up residential garbage. We lived on one of his garbage routes on Hickory Street near the lower campus of Mankato State University (known now as Minnesota State University at Mankato).

In the sixties Dutch Lyons loved to market his Mankato, Minnesota business, and one of the ways he did this was to wear white pants, shirt, and a white cap as he went about his garbage pick-up business.

He painted red-lettered statements on his white garbage trucks like, "Our Business is Picking Up," and "Double Your Garbage Back if You're Not Satisfied with Our Business." He was a self-proclaimed "garbologist," and was the first one that I ever heard using that term. He was a funny guy and had achieved regional notoriety when he had appeared on the Johnny Carson Television Show.

There are steep hills in the city of Mankato as the Minnesota River has flowed through there for a couple of million years. When I got Dutch on the phone, I said nothing is moving in this part of town, but if he could pick me up I'd buy him lunch at Michael's, the only open restaurant in town.

He said his garbage trucks were high off the ground, and he thought he could make it to the top of Hickory Street, where we lived. It was a moderately steep hill near the lower campus of Mankato State University.

After about thirty minutes of waiting and watching, I had given up on Dutch being able to get through the snow. I decided that I would review my lesson plans for the novel, *The Catcher in the Rye*, which I was teaching to my junior English students. Shortly thereafter, a truck horn blasted away my concentration, and I looked out of the window and there was Dutch, wearing his white cap and smiling.

It was the first and the last time that I ever went to lunch in a garbage truck, and it was a unique way to spend part of an education snow day in Minnesota.

Monthly Beer Runs

After high school, I had quit college twice, had worked a little over a year as a laborer for a plumbing contractor, served two years in the U.S. Army, and graduated from Mankato State University with a bachelor's degree in speech and English.

In 1966 my first teacher's contract with the Waterville-Elysian School District was for 4900 dollars a year; and with two class plays and as the director of declamation activities, it sky-rocketed to an annual salary of 5250 dollars. I also picked up a couple of hundred bucks a year as an assistant high school wrestling coach.

At age twenty-seven and my second year of teaching, my teacher colleagues had asked me to be their representative in contract negotiations with the school board. I think that their choice of me was due more to the fact that no one else wanted to do the task than it was their confidence in me as a negotiator.

I met frequently with the board and superintendent on contract matters and reported the progress, or lack thereof, to the teachers periodically. When we had concluded the negotiations, I had gotten them the largest percentage raise and dollar amount in the history of that school district. Was this due to my extraordinary negotiations skills or due to the beginning of extraordinary inflationary times? I think the latter.

After the last negotiation meeting, one of the school board members asked me if I wanted to go downtown for a beer. I said sure and I met a couple of the board members at the Corner Bar in Waterville, and the beer-buying barrier was broken.

Prior to that time, all of the teachers who drank bought their beer or liquor out of town. Some of us would make a beer run on the monthly payday to a neighboring small town. After that Corner Bar "breaking-the-local-bar barrier" with some school board members, we concluded that it was an endorsement for us to buy our beer and liquor supplies in town, although we usually went through the back door.

I left that district at the end of that year for a new position in the Minneapolis suburb of Robbinsdale and would not deal with small town issues again until the last two years of my career.

"Who Dun nit?"

Wally Lymburn was the Waterville-Elysian High School principal, and he had an office on the second floor of the three-story building. Most of us called him Wally. There were teacher mailboxes in an area next to Wally's office, with ditto and stencil machines for the teachers to use. My classroom was on the third floor so I usually stopped by to check my mail on the way to my classroom.

Wally and I both smoked in the boiler room in the basement before we went upstairs at the beginning of the day. We usually enjoyed an early morning cup of coffee and a cigarette in that crummy space. There was an old couch and a couple of wooden chairs and Perry Pope, the head custodian, was usually there too. Perry Pope didn't smoke but he liked to be part of the conversation. He was a good ol' guy.

One morning I stopped by the "lounge" and neither Perry nor Wally was there. I had a quick cup of coffee and a smoke and headed upstairs. When I got to the door that led into Wally's office and the mail room, I noticed that the door glass was broken and there were still shards of broken glass on the floor.

Then I spotted Wally and the Sheriff and I said, "Hey Wally, what's up?"

He responded, "I can't talk now; I'll see you later in the lounge." He smiled slyly and had a twinkle in his eyes.

About twenty minutes later and still a full thirty minutes until school started, I headed down to our "smokers' lounge." I was curious as to who had broken into the principal's office and what they had taken.

Wally was seated at one end of the old couch puffing on a cigarette as I stood in the middle of the small room lighting up one of my Pall

Mall's that I stashed on a corner shelf. Wally had a big grin on his face as I asked, "What was stolen and did he know who the burglar was?"

He said the crooks had broken into his office and had taken the petty cash of about twenty-five dollars out of a small cash box located in a three-drawer filing cabinet.

I had an English minor and I heard him say the plural crooks. Again I asked, "Do you know who they were?" The suspense was killing me, and Perry the head custodian, who had appeared out of nowhere, was all ears.

Principal Wally was going to get all the mileage he could out of his knowing who the burglars were. "Yes, we know who they are," Wally stated.

"Ah ha, so do you know how many there were?"

Wally blew a bad smoke ring and stated, "There were three of them."

"Did you catch them red-handed?"

"Nope."

"Well then, how do you know who they are?" I inquired. Wally was starting to piss me off in his smug kind of way. Silent Perry had a big grin on his face and just sat on the couch taking it all in. Perry would be the conduit to the public, and he couldn't wait to get out and tell the school bus drivers.

"Well," Wally said as he pulled long on his Camel cigarette and started floating bad smoke rings across the dead room, "We have a pretty good idea who they are."

The suspense was killing me and Wally reminded me of some bad Hollywood actor drawing out a death scene, and I said, "Alright goddamn it, Wally, if you didn't catch them red-handed, how do you know who they are?"

Wally was proud as a peacock, sucked in a big draw on his weed, puffed out his chest, and he continued, "Alright, alright, keep your pants on. Apparently, in the heat of their crime, they got hot, took off their athletic letter jackets and threw them in a pile. Something or someone must have startled them, and they made a quick exit leaving their letter jackets in a pile. As you know, their names are on their letter jackets."

"Not the smartest crooks you'll ever run across," I said. Perry Pope slapped his leg. Wally snuffed out his cigarette in a sand-filled bucket, nodded yes, and headed upstairs to accept the best actor award and continue his day as the high school principal and major criminal sleuth.

Perry looked at me and said, "Not the smartest crooks you'll ever run across," and was off to spread the news.

"Right," I said and I headed off to class wondering who didn't have their letter jackets on that day.

I left the school district that year but I never did find out who the "hot" robbers were or "who dun nit?" To my knowledge, there was never any public disclosure about the "mystery bandits," the crime, nor the punishment.

The Nineteen Seventies

The Model Room

Lyle Mottinger was the principal at Hosterman Junior High School, one of three junior high schools in the Robbinsdale school district. That junior high school had approximately twelve hundred students and was located in Crystal, Minnesota, a second tier suburb northwest of Minneapolis. Lyle had asked me to come see him at the end of my teaching day. It was a fine spring day in May, 1972.

At about 3 p.m., I was standing at the counter and I couldn't help overhearing a distraught mother complaining to Mr. Mottinger in his office. Mottinger's secretary told me that they had been meeting for approximately fifteen minutes before I came.

"Mr. Mottinger, you've got to stop those monster boys from pounding on my car when I come after school to pick up my kids."

"Yes, Mrs. Miller, I will do that if you will just please tell me where exactly this takes place."

"I park right next to the elementary school on Winnetka Avenue and my two sons walk the block from Hosterman because I pick up my daughter at the elementary school."

"Okay, now once again please tell me what kind of car that you drive; and I'll hide out down there and catch the boys who you say are pounding on your car. Now, please tell me the make of your car and the color."

"I can't do that."

"Mrs. Miller, if you don't tell me what the model car is and what the color is, how will I know which car to look for?"

"Just watch for some boys beating on a car's hood."

"Winnetka Avenue is a very busy street, especially at the close of the school day. I don't understand why you won't give me a description of your car."

"I can't tell you the make and color of the car that I'm driving."

"Do you have that many cars?"

"No, but each day I drive a different car."

"Oh, I see. Does your husband own or work at a used car lot?"

"No, No, why are you making this so hard for me?"

"I'm sorry, Mrs. Miller, but I'm just trying to establish with you the color and make of your car. Is this so hard for you to tell me? If telling me this basic information is so difficult for you, I just won't be able to help you in this matter."

Mrs. Miller began to cry. "I just can't have our cars damaged."

He came out of his office and grabbed a box of Kleenex off the counter and rolled his eyes and eyebrows upward. "I understand, Mrs. Miller. Relax, try to control yourself and tell me what you want me to do."

"I just (sob) want you to (sob) catch those boys (sob) and keep my (sob) husband from yelling (sob) at me."

"Why is he yelling at you?"

"Because a couple of the cars that I have driven have been dented."

"Mrs. Miller, I think you need to share with me what is going on here or else I will be unable to help you."

"My husband owns a gas station down on 42nd Street (sob). A lot of his customers work in buildings where they drop their car off for minor repairs when they go to work and then pick it up at the end of their work day. All we own is a pickup truck and it's pretty small to pick up the children after school. (Sob) So I go over to the gas station and take one of the cars that have been serviced and use it to pick up our kids. It has been working just fine the past couple of years until this week."

"I'll go down to Winnetka Avenue for a couple of days and see if I can catch the boys, Mrs. Miller."

"Thank you, Mr. Mottinger. And, please don't tell anyone about the cars I use."

"Our conversation will remain confidential, Mrs. Miller. Now, I have another appointment unless you have something else you would like to discuss with me."

"No, sir. Thank you, Mr. Mottinger."

"Goodbye, Mrs. Miller." (Mrs. Miller exits stage left.)

Lyle Mottinger was a no-nonsense principal and he ran a tight ship. I liked and respected him, and he had a staff of fun-loving people, most were in their twenties and thirties. He had a good sense of humor, but I don't think that he socialized with many of the staff outside of school functions.

Lyle had an assistant principal named Larry Villars who meted out a lot of discipline to unruly students. He was a commander in the Navy Reserve and knew how to discipline the Navy way. Villars once told me that one of his heros, the late John F. Kennedy had said, "Always forgive your enemies—just before you hang them." To my knowledge, Villars never hanged any of the students. Larry had a bad back and he had a rocking chair in his office, ala John Kennedy; and when he wasn't in that rocking chair, the staff said behind his back that "Villars was off his rocker."

I knew no one who ever talked disparagingly of Lyle Mottinger the three years that I taught at Hosterman. There was a whole lot of unexplained "staff-chemistry" at Hosterman Junior High School, and I never experienced any school/college atmosphere close to that atmosphere over the next thirty years.

In the sixties, all male teachers and administrators wore suits or sports coats, ties and I never saw Lyle Mottinger without his suit or sports coat on at work. I remember that Lyle was a sharp dresser, had a short flattop haircut, which even in the sixties was rather rare, and he wore a class ring on his middle finger.

Lyle came out of his office following Mrs. Miller, who had bloodshot eyes. He invited me into his office.

"Nate, thanks for stopping by. I'd like to talk with you about a plan that I have for dealing with some potential ninth-grade drop-outs."

"Say, Lyle, how about that Mrs. Miller? Was she nuts or what did she expect you to do about those kids, the borrowed cars, and her dilemma?"

"Well, you know, Nate, we have to deal with a lot of different situations; but let's talk about why I've asked you to come see me today."

"Sounds good to me."

"Nate, you've been with us at Hosterman a couple of years as a teacher and a football coach. You've been an emcee at some of our social events and most of the staff just loves you. What I'm about to ask you is to take a totally different direction and help us keep some kids in school who are high-risk potential drop-out students. We have the feeling that if we can keep them in school, they will have a better chance of success after high school. We don't want these kids to drop out of school before or after ninth grade."

"Lyle, I have a major in speech and a minor in English. How do I fit into this scheme?"

"Nate, we think that you have the kind of personality that can work with special-needs kids and help them to stay in school. They need someone who is firm, but able to accept their complex behaviors."

"Lyle, why do you think that I would be that kind of teacher?"

"We have watched you over the past couple of years. We know that you have spent a number of hours on your own time observing special education teachers in their classrooms and that you have told those teachers how fascinated you have been with their teaching strategies."

"Wow, I had no idea that you knew that I was doing that."

"We probably know more about you than you think, Nate. "

"I'll tell you this, Lyle, I know more about teaching now after watching those special education teachers than I knew before I came here."

"That's great, Nate. Now, I want to tell you why I've called you in here today. We have a number of kids who drop out every year as soon as they reach sixteen, the minimum age for officially being able to drop out of school in Minnesota. We think that you can help us save some of these kids and keep them in school. Would you be willing to help us do that?"

"Yes, but please tell me more."

"We've got this idea that if we kept some of these problem students in a contained area and gave them their basic education that they might be able to succeed."

"I'm bewildered; how could I help achieve that?"

"We have this concept of a 'Model Room.' By 'Model Room,' we're talking about creating an environment where students would start in a self-contained classroom for the whole day, except for health and physical education classes. In the self-contained classroom, they would be taught English, science, social studies, math, and they would be out of the classroom for phys-ed and health.

"But, Lyle, I'm only licensed to teach in English and speech."

"I've had some conversations with some people at the state department of education, and I think I can get you some waivers for some of the teaching licenses because of the experimental nature of this idea. If you're interested, I will give you some paid preparation time this summer to work on the curriculum. I will also give you access to teachers and consultants as you prepare a curriculum model for this program."

"It really sounds interesting, Lyle. But I don't know if I have the qualifications to pull this off. May I have a few days to think it over before I give you my answer?"

"Absolutely, Nate. You think it over and talk with others about the idea and then get back to me as soon as you can. Thanks for coming in, Nate. I really believe that you have the talent and skills to pull this thing off."

"Thanks for your confidence in me, Lyle. I'll be back to see you when I've made a decision."

I talked the idea over with my wife, some teacher friends, the school counselors and the school social worker. I went in and saw Lyle Mottinger a few days later and told him I'd try it for one year. He received the necessary teacher-license approvals from the state department of education, although I never saw them. That was a very busy summer for me working on curriculum for the "Model Room" ninth graders as well as going to graduate school classes. The principal, counselors, and social worker spent part of their summer selecting the students for the program and meeting with the parents of the students.

I started the fall quarter with seventeen students in the Model Room. For a "normal" classroom that would have been an ideal class size. For that experiment, there were too many students. The students all had years of behavior problems documented in their records so the first few weeks were just plain hell for me. Not having complete control of a classroom setting was a new experience for me in that Model Classroom.

Dave, our school social worker, helped me resolve the lack of classroom control with some basic in-service education for me. He gave me practical verbal and written information about positive behavior modification. I then set about the task of creating a daily tally sheet of behaviors that I wanted to reinforce. I shared my progress with the social worker for his critique and he was extremely helpful. As I recall the general positive reinforcement areas included areas such as the following for the students:

Focus on the lesson
Lesson participation
Socials skills with other students
Use of appropriate school language
Attendance
Punctuality
Behavior (in classroom)
Behavior (outside of classroom)
Completion of assignments
Attitude
Appearance
Cooperation
Values Clarification

Each student could daily earn from one to five points in each of the areas. I needed to be focused all of the time since I needed to award points in thirteen-plus areas for all seventeen students. It was a time-consuming process. I learned quickly to notice and record the behaviors as I saw them occur, which saved me valuable time at the end of the day. Once the program was implemented, the first thing that the students wanted to know the next classroom day was how many points they had earned the previous day.

What did they do with the points? The points enabled the students to buy privileges that they normally would not get. Each student was given the list of activities that they could buy with their points and I also had the list posted in a couple places around the classroom. For some of the activities, I needed to make special arrangements so they needed to let me know the day before. There were many activities that they could buy and as I recall some of them were

Chewing gum
Making a phone call on a public phone in the hallway
Running in-school errands for me
Taking a nap at their desk
Playing a game inside the classroom; such as checkers, chess, etcetera.

For games requiring more than one player, each player had to spend points in order to play

Reading an appropriate magazine that they brought to class

Reading books, magazines, newspapers that we furnished

Listening to a radio or phonograph record with a headset

Watching television or a film at the audio visual department

Each of the purchased privileges had a designated purchase price. The more independence that the purchase permitted the greater was the cost. Within two weeks of implementation of the positive reinforcement plan, I had those kids in the palms of my hands. Working with all of those "troubled" kids became enjoyable and I looked forward to going to work. The plan worked beautifully and I used it for the entire year. One of the boys hardly used any of his earned points. I guess he was just proud of his point accumulation; and by the end of the year, he had approximately 7500 points remaining.

One day early in the winter of that year, one of those fifteen-year-old boys had bought a gum-chewing privilege. During an independent study time, he came up to me and said, "Here, Mr. J., have a stick of gum." Normally, I refused those kinds of offers, but that day I accommodated Jared's gesture and accepted the stick of gum. A short time later, I was walking around the classroom checking on the independent workers when I began to feel a stirring in my stomach. I quickly swallowed the gum, which was an error. I knew at that time that I had been tricked and given some kind of gum laxative.

Jared looked at me and said, "How you doing, Mr. J?"

"Just fine, is there some reason why I shouldn't feel fine?"

"No, sir. I was just asking."

There were still twenty-five minutes until we all went to lunch. It was one of the few times during the day when I could be away from the room and be with other adults. I never left the room unsupervised because I knew that there was always the potential for something to go wrong. I wanted to go to the bathroom, but I decided I could hold out until lunch time. If I would have let the students go to lunch early they would have known that they had gotten to me. I made it until lunch and to the men's room before I exploded. As I sat there, I was cursing Jared. I spent my entire half hour in the men's room without any lunch. When I went back to open up the classroom, Jared was

111

right there inquiring with a big grin on his face, "How was lunch, Mr. J?"

"It was just great. My wife made me an extraordinary lunch and thanks for asking." I would not let them have the pleasure of knowing just how much that they had gotten to me. I never took any gum or anything else from those students again.

Hosterman Junior High was a one-story building with one wing each for the seventh, eighth, and ninth grades. There was also a home economics and industrial arts wing. In the middle of that configuration, there were the band and vocal programs, physical education gyms, swimming pool, and audio visual department. From one end of a wing to the opposite end was probably one-to-two city blocks. In order to save time for minor repairs, the custodians rode bicycles when classes were in session. One time I needed a tool to repair something in the Model Room and I sent Jeff to get the tool from a custodian. The custodians' work area was at the opposite end of the building near the industrial arts wing. What I didn't know was that they had a secured work closet in each of the wings. When Jeff was back in short order, I figured that he had run into one of the custodians and gotten the tool and had returned to the classroom. He had not. I found our much later that Jeff's dad was a lock-smith and apparently had taught Jeff some of the tools of the trade. Jeff had just picked the lock in the nearest custodial work room.

Every one of my Model Room freshman entered Cooper High School the following year. Both the students and I learned a lot that year in the Model Room. I only worked in that Model Room for one year because I accepted a similar type position at Robbinsdale High School as a Work Experience Teacher-Coordinator, working primarily with juniors and seniors with similar problems at the high school level.

Rotten Tomatoes

As any gardener knows at the end of the vegetable growing season tomatoes left on the vine get pretty rotten. And so it was in the fall of the year when my son Jay and his neighborhood buddy Scott decided to take some of those rotten tomatoes and throw them at some passing motorists on County Road 30 in the city of Maple Grove, Minnesota.

The speed limit along County Road thirty was fifty-five miles per hour, so to actually hit one of the moving vehicles for a couple ten-year-olds would be difficult, at best. The first car that they hurled their soggy tomatoes at, they hit broad-side. The driver slammed on the brakes and the boys took off for cover behind our house, which was approximately two hundred feet from where they had scored a direct hit. They took refuge behind some four-foot high bushes that were right next to the back of our house.

The police officer driving the squad car that had just been hit with some slimy tomatoes had slammed on the brakes, made an abrupt u-turn and saw the boys going behind our house. The police officer often brought me agenda for the City of Maple Grove City Council Meetings, since I was a member of that governing body. He told me later that he had roared into our driveway, bringing the car to a screeching halt, and set off in pursuit of the boys. He told me that when he went around the back corner of our house, he nearly started laughing when he saw the boys crouched down and hiding behind a big bush with no leaves on it.

The officer told me later that he got them to stand up and thoroughly chewed them out. The boys were repenting their dastardly deed as the tears streamed down their faces. They had received a stern warning from the police officer, but would not do any jail time. Later the officer and I had quite a laugh about their conspicuous hiding place, without their presence, of course.

113

Stolen Payroll Checks and the FBI

As a teacher at Robbinsdale High School, a first tier suburb located on the northwest side of Minneapolis, I worked with a group of high school students who were at high risk for dropping out of school. I worked with them in the classroom on career development skills, values clarification, socialization skills without alcohol or drugs, and job searching skills. In the afternoon, I visited with them and their bosses on the job.

As a kind of respite from the daily grind of dealing with behavior problem kids, I had volunteered to be an advisor to a group of boys in a Key Club. Key Club was sponsored by and affiliated with the Kiwanis Clubs. This was a group of approximately fifteen of the finest young men that you will ever run across. They were positive oriented towards doing voluntary good deeds in the school and in the community. They were an absolute joy to work with.

I had just returned from a conference for the Key Club boys in Aberdeen, South Dakota, and it was a Sunday afternoon. My wife said I was to call a vice president of the Crystal State Bank upon my arrival home. We had our checking and savings accounts at that bank. I called the bank vice president and he wanted to know if I had made deposits of several thousand dollars on the previous Friday. I said absolutely not, and he asked me to come down to the bank on Monday to talk with him further about this. I said I most certainly would.

The next day I went down to the bank during my preparation period at the high school. Stolen payroll checks from a business in

114

Georgia had been deposited in our account amounting to several thousand dollars. One of my deposit slips had been used and quite possibly it had been found in a garbage dumpster; I really didn't know. Furthermore, in those times stores and banks had generic checks that you could draft if you did not have your personal checks with you at the time (although that convenience disappeared decades ago). What the crooks had done was write checks for several thousand dollars at the bank; and when the teller had checked our account balance, there was plenty of money to cover the checks (the stolen payroll check deposits had inflated my account balance).

The bank vice president then took me and introduced me to each of the dozen or so tellers explaining that I was the real Nathan Johnson. It was a little late then. The bank VP explained that since this involved interstate crime that the FBI would be involved in the investigation and would be contacting me. Later that day, I received a phone call from an FBI agent out of the Minneapolis field office who set up an appointment with me at our home for the next day.

I made the appointment for 4 p.m. because I wanted my two elementary children to see an FBI agent so that they could talk about it in school. At precisely 4 p.m., a plain black car pulled into our driveway in Maple Grove, Minnesota, and two FBI agents approached the front door. They looked just as they did in the movies at that time wearing three-piece dark suits and neat haircuts, but they were very young. The boys were standing right behind me when the agents rang the doorbell. I asked them for identification so that the boys could see their badges and I invited them in. I offered them soft drinks, which they politely refused, and the three of us sat around the dining room table with one boy on each side of me taking all of this in with wide-eyed excitement.

The agents had a three-ring notebook with several pieces of evidence covered with plastic sheet protectors. They asked me to review their evidence and compared my signature to those of the crooks and they were as unrelated as they could be. They told me the basic story that the bank VP had told me except they thought that a similar occurrence had also occurred in Brooklyn Park, another suburb close to Crystal, Minnesota (these suburbs are second-ring suburbs to the northwest of Minneapolis).

I would estimate that the FBI agents were at the house less than twenty minutes and I heard from them about ten days later that they had caught the culprits and that the robbers' fingerprints had matched those on the stolen payroll checks, deposit slips, etcetera. I was amazed that they could do that kind of investigative work in the seventies.

Watergate and the Russian Ambassador

I accompanied the Key Club to the national conference in Washington D.C. in June of 1972. Those young men really needed no chaperone and it was a privilege for me to be with them. I had been an advisor to local, regional, and national leadership conferences for high school groups other than the Key Club. Those other conferences had all required around-the-clock monitoring for potential behavioral problems (and believe me, we had a number of situations when students were sent home immediately from the conference). That was never a case with the Key Club boys.

In the lobby of the Washington Hilton, waiting for a tour bus to Mt. Vernon, I remember watching a television newscast that included an announcement of an early morning break-in at the Watergate Complex on June 17, 1972. On a tour the day before the break-in at the Watergate Complex, we drove by the complex. The tour director announced to the partial Minnesota group of Key Club members, "Senator Hubert H. Humphrey and his wife Murial live here." I was unimpressed by the look of the structure from the outside as we drove past it. The Watergate Complex consisted of offices, apartments, a hotel, and exclusive retail stores.

I was amused by the tour driver who had an eloquent voice, but was obviously lacking in some of his language skills. On one occasion as we were crossing over a river bridge, he explained that the Potomac was full of, as he explained it, "deb-riss." Most of us would recognize the word as debris (dub-ree). Good Key Club members, however, would never openly be critical of someone's error.

On the grounds of Mt. Vernon, I was particularly impressed with the thick hedges that surrounded that magnificent estate of our first President. I was elated in the gift shop to be able to pick up a small potted plant that I could take home to try to replicate those wonderful hedges. When the sales clerk was about to ring up my purchases, one of which was a small hedge plant, I said, "Are these plants hardy?"

"Absolutely, if it never gets below forty degrees above Fahrenheit."

I laughed politely and said, "It often gets forty degrees below Fahrenheit in Minnesota."

She graciously replied, "The plant will have difficulty growing and I would recommend that you not purchase it if you want to plant it back home." I asked the salesperson to return the potted plant and purchased my other souvenirs.

That night we went to a new musical with the Gagnons, Tom and Julie, from New Hope, Minnesota, who were chaperones for the Key Club from Cooper High School in Robbinsdale. The show was being performed near the Kennedy Center; it was *Jesus Christ Super Star*. I was the "Lone Ranger" in the group in my appreciation of that play, since I did not fully appreciate the music or the lyrics of the show as the other three in our group. I thought that Andrew Lloyd Weber's musical had gone over the line.

We were told the day before that we would have a Russian Ambassador speak to the group of approximately 1000 Key Club members from around the nation at our final group session on Friday at 9 a.m. at the Washington Hilton. I told the boys that we should meet at the auditorium of the hotel by 8:15 if we wanted to get good seats. At 8:15 we were fifty feet from the doors, and I wondered if we would get a decent seat. We ended up nearly half-way back from the stage. I was disappointed at first, but my positive-oriented wife said, "What if we had arrived at 9 a.m.?"

The emcee made a nice introduction for the Russian Ambassador and the Key Club boys gave him a rousing round of applause. With a heavy accent, he began telling us that things weren't so "hot" in America.

He held up a copy of the *New York Times* and said, "Look at this on page one; they are still looking for a serial killer who has raped and killed seven women in New York City. It must not be safe to be out doors in that city after dark. And look at this, a big banker is under investigation for fraud. So much for the free enterprise system. And on page two, they are telling you that inflation is nearing fifteen percent and that there may be a gas war this summer. There may not be any gasoline left for you boys when you go home to cruise up and down Main Street in your big high-powered cars. What do you think of that, boys?" It was a rhetorical question, but I heard a few muffled comments near me.

The ambassador continued as he held up a copy of the *Los Angeles Times*. "Look at this. It says there was another night of riots in Los Angeles and the police commissioner has placed an extra 3500 cops on night watch. And here I thought this was a peaceful country. This would not happen in the USSR."

The boys were beginning to stir in their seats.

The Russian Ambassador stood about six-foot-two, weighed approximately two hundred and seventy-five pounds, had silver hair, and had on a striking black pin-striped three-piece suit. The suit was obviously silk, and he looked like the bankers on Wall Street.

The ambassador continued with his harangue on articles in the *Los Angles Times*: "Here is an article, boys, about how under paid the farm workers are in the great state of California. Your free enterprise system rewards the rich and robs the poor. I guess that's why you love Robin Hood in the move picture shows. In Russia, we take care of our farm workers."

More stirring in the audience. My wife said softly to me, "Why is he doing this?"

I replied, "I don't know; it doesn't seem appropriate for this group."

Ambassador holding up a copy of the *Washington* Post, "Here's a story, boys, about some burglars breaking into the Watergate Complex this week. That's a pretty expensive apartment complex where rent averages about 150,000 dollars a year. I understand that a number of United States Senators live there. Maybe those burglars were after some of their hard-earned and corrupt money."

"I've heard enough," one of the boys said softly behind me. I turned and put my forefinger to my lips to squelch further remarks.

The ambassador ranted on, "Here's another *Post* article about a United States Congressman skinny-dipping in a fountain with a prostitute. Is that the kind of people that you elect to represent you in Washington, D. C.?"

The boys were getting restless and there were conversations going on all over the place. One Key Club boy, about four rows in front of us, stood up and shouted, "Mr. Ambassador, I'd like to make a comment and then ask you a question."

The startled ambassador stopped in the middle of his sentence and said, "Do you think you can interrupt the USSR Ambassador to the United States in the middle of an important speech?"

The lad responded with an accent typical of New England, "You are painting a pretty dismal picture of the greatest and longest standing democracy in the world."

"Not true, young man; you're wrong. I'm only showing life as it exists in America."

"Not true, Mr. Ambassador. I could give you positive examples of stewardship, citizenship, love, and democratic principles of success that will demonstrate to you what we truly are."

"Enough, I didn't come here to have you preach to me. What is your question?"

"You have held up newspapers from three great cities in the United States and shared negative news stories. I admit that those stories may represent a segment of our society. My question for you is 'Why don't you have freedom of the press in Russia?'"

"Young man, either you are an idiot, you are misinformed, or both."

More audience stirring, some sporadic applause, and the comments are becoming more vocal from this teenage crowd, "Answer the question."

"Leave him alone."

"Who does this guy think he is?"

"Mr. Ambassador, if your idea of freedom of the press in Russia is the state-run *Pravda*, you have answered my question."

Cheers and applause by the audience.

The Ambassador was yelling into the microphone to resume control, "You, young man, are a victim of either brainwashing, propaganda, or both. Our people in my homeland have a right to express their views anytime. Our government does not interfere with the operation of the newspaper *Pravda*. "

By now there were perhaps fifty, of one thousand boys, standing around the ballroom of the Washington Hilton. They were waving their hands and trying to get the attention of the ambassador.

The ambassador reluctantly pointed at a thin, typically blue-blazer gray-slack Key Club boy about seventy feet away from us, who shouted, "What about your secret police?"

Ambassador, "What about your FBI?"

My wife said to me, "I think this is getting out of control."

I replied, "I think that something else is going on, but I can't put my finger on it."

Another boy shouted, "How come people can't leave your country freely?"

"You boys are making me angry and I'm tired of your stupid questions. I came here in good faith to talk to you today, and you have shown no respect to me. You have belittled my country and embarrassed me."

It was at that time that I heard a song starting in the back of the room and the verse was oh so familiar. Soon a young male audience in excess of 1000 was standing on their feet and singing, "God Bless America." I was so touched by the singing that tears were running down my face and I said to my wife, "I think we've been had."

The ambassador had raised the newspapers and thrown them on the floor and stormed off the stage. The emcee had reemerged and was raising his hands trying to quiet the crowd as the second refrain of "God Bless America" was drawing to a close.

The emcee calmed everybody down and got us all seated and then explained what had just happened. He brought the "bogus" Russian Ambassador back and re-introduced him as a New York actor. The actor explained to us that his purpose was to show us how angry and excited we could become by someone who knew how to get to us. He through the use of words had accomplished his purpose. He also told us that when he had done a similar program at a Marine Corp base in California that the marines had charged the stage and he had to run for his life.

It was a great lesson for all of us present to reflect on how untrue the old rhyme was, "Sticks and stones may break my bones but words can never hurt me." The message was clear that speeches can be both negative and positive motivators. As listeners we need to focus not only on the message, but also on the messenger.

Skamper's Muffled Bark

We had a household pet dog for seventeen years named Skamper. He had the coal black curly hair typical of a breed called "Wire-Haired Terriers." He was not a pure-bred, and he never weighed more than fifteen pounds, but he was fearless. One time, I remember that he raced out after a Doberman Pincher, clearly sixty pounds over Skamper's weight, who Skamper thought was invading his territory. That dog would have had Skamper for lunch had the Doberman not been on a leash and under the control of his owner while walking past our house. What Skamper lacked in "common-sense" he made up for in courage.

Late one fall afternoon in 1974, I had just arrived home from my teaching job, and I was sitting down reading the daily newspaper. An opportunity to read the daily news paper was a relaxing time of the day for me. My wife wasn't home from work at that time, and my elementary school-aged boys were playing a pick-up game of football in the back yard with some neighbor boys. I had taken off my shoes and was pretty absorbed in my reading, when I heard a couple thumps on the back of the house.

The dining room drapes were pulled in front of the sliding patio door, so I cranked open the kitchen window above the sink and yelled out to the boys, "Be careful with that football. We don't want any broken windows."

And as you would expect they responded that they were being careful and not to worry about the windows.

I had just resumed my reading when I heard a couple more thumps on the house. I got up and went back to the window and said, "Hey, I just told you guys to be careful with that football. Now, you're hitting the house again!"

122

They said they were innocent and that the football hadn't come close to hitting the house. As a high school teacher, I gave myself a multiple choice question:

A. Do they think that I'm deaf?

B. Do they think I'm an idiot? Or,

C. Do they think both of the above?"

I decided that I could play this game too, so I walked away from the window and stood in the hallway. The next time that they hit the house, I would catch them and do what, I wasn't quite certain. I stood there no more than a minute, in my best Sherlock Holmes persona, when I heard a *thump-thump* on the patio door.

I sprang into action and in a flash, I pulled open the patio door drapes, slid open the sliding patio door, and said "gotcha!"

And what to my startled eyes did appear, but Skamper, our dog, with his head stuck inside a gallon glass jar. Yes, a gallon-glass jar.

I quickly picked him up. Somehow, he had gotten outside and had been roaming the neighborhood when he had spied some treasure in the bottom of that jar.

The boys came running when they heard me yell "gotcha" and saw Skamper in the jar in my arms.

I could not get the jar off his head as I sat on the floor with my necktie loosened, no shoes on, the newspaper all over the dining room floor, and a bunch of small boys huddled around me exclaiming, "Skamper is going to die! Skamper is going to die!" I didn't know what to do.

Again, I tried to get the jar off of his head; but it was on there too tight. I could get a forefinger between his neck and the top of the jar, so I figured some oxygen was getting in there. Plus there had to have been some oxygen in the jar before he had jammed his head into the jar for the great treasure.

Still holding the dog, which seemed to be breathing okay in spite of the jar on its head but still giving an occasional muffled bark, I called a teacher friend of mine. Jo Campe raised dogs and I thought he might be able to tell me what to do. Luckily, he was home. I told him about my dilemma. I inquired if I should break the glass jar on Skamper's head with a hammer. And he said, "No, broken glass might get in Skamper's eyes or ears." He recommended taking Skamper to a veterinarian.

I hung up the phone and decided to take his advice. The dog seemed to be breathing harder, so I thought I have to get to the vet in a hurry.

I was afraid to put the dog down because I thought he might strike the jar on one of the wrought-iron dining room chairs that were popular at the time. So I jumped in the old Ford, holding Skamper on my lap, with no shoes on, and set out for the vet clinic, which was about five miles away.

I know that I exceeded the speed limit driving to the vet, but I felt certain that I could have gained the sympathy of any cop who stopped me when he saw the dog in my lap with the space-age glass jar on his head. The inside of the jar had a light layer of moisture, like steam from Skamper's breathing. I was beginning to think that he was going to smother.

When I walked into the vet clinic and placed Skamper on the counter, the receptionist with eyes wide-open exclaimed, "How did that happen?"

I shrugged and said, "I don't know, but we need to get it off quickly."

She got the vet who laughed when he saw the dog and said, "Now there's a first." (Vets usually don't have a lot to say.)

We took Skamper into one of their exam rooms and tried to wiggle the jar off of his head. When that didn't work, they gave him a sedative. When the dog was relaxed, they applied some Vaseline around his neck and with a little time gently pulled the jar over his head.

The doctor did a quick examination and looked at me with a twinkle in his eye and said, "I never cared much for pickled pigs-feet."

"Me neither," I responded.

Pickled pigs-feet, according to the label, was what had been in the jar that Skamper was after. As I drove home I wondered, *who in my neighborhood bought pickled pigs-feet by the gallon?*

Skamper lived some fourteen years after that incident; and as far as I know, he never stuck his head into another gallon jar. It was probably his first and last taste of pickled pigs-feet. I still have not had my first taste.

I got the veterinarian's bill for sixty-five dollars for Skamper's visit a couple days later. At that time, an office call for me was only thirty-five dollars in a physician's office. But then, I never had gone into my doctor's office with a gallon jar on my head.

A Shortened Tie and Banana Cream Pie

One of my friends at Robbinsdale High School was Jerry Davis who was a Distributive Education Teacher Coordinator. I had a similar position a couple of years later at Armstrong High School, a sister school in the Robbinsdale School District. There were six of us in the vocational-technical education department at Robbinsdale High School. The other members of our department were Clotile Pease, Fred Geisler, Jerry Davis, Dick Demeuling, and Joe Pucel. We took over some abandoned storage space in the basement. We scavenged around and found a bunch of partially used cans of paint and mixed them all together. We painted our new office space, scrounged up some old furniture, and we had our "new" office area.

The high school principal was a man named Robert Ferrell, who spent a lot of his time in his office with the door closed. He claimed on many occasions that he had an "open door policy," but most of the staff just laughed and talked about his weak leadership skills. To show the principal what they thought of his "open door policy," two wrestling coaches took his office door off its hinges and walked into a faculty meeting and placed it up next to him as the staff cheered. Robbinsdale High School had an enrollment exceeding 2400 students in grades tenth through twelfth. There was an unwritten rule that only male coaches sat at the south end of the faculty lounge. I wasn't a coach, but I sat there whenever I felt like it and I was never intimidated by any coach.

The faculty lounge always seemed to be a hot spot for negative conversations about other staff, school administrators, or President

Nixon. One time a male counselor and I made up a small sign and erected it on one of the tables in the lounge and it read, "Positive Conversation Only at This Table." After about a week of isolation at the table, we took the sign down. Not one person had joined us.

Back to Jerry Davis, he was a bachelor, an air force navigation officer in the air force reserve, a sharp dresser, and about my age. We had a lot in common and laughed at similar things. Jerry's desk and mine abutted because of cramped office space. One morning, I looked across at Jerry. He had on a light blue suit, a white shirt, and a tie. I said, "Jerry, that's a real sharp suit."

"Thanks."

"That's the ugliest tie, however, that I have ever seen. Are those pheasants in flight on that tie?"

"They sure are and this is a beautiful tie," Jerry responded and went back to his work.

I don't know what got into me, but I reached into my desk drawer and pulled out my scissors. I took about three steps and grabbed his tie and cut it off at about the middle of the tie. Jerry looked up astonished and said, "What will Fran say?"

Fran Dobbs was his fiancée and I said, "Why do you bring up Fran's name?"

"She made this tie for me." By that time, he had taken the knot out of the remainder of the tie and laid it on his desk.

I felt like the biggest jerk on the face of the earth; and to add insult to injury, I took the two pieces of the tie and stapled them together. I began to wonder how I would ever make up for that stupid prank to Jerry and Fran. Fran was a lovely person who worked as a registered nurse.

Fran and Jerry would remind me every once in a while about the pheasant tie. After about two years, Jerry confessed to me that Fran had not made the tie and that it was just his quick response when I had cut off his tie. I appreciated the confession and congratulated him on his quick thinking at the time of the incident. Whenever I went tie shopping, as I always had a lot of ties, I would look for one with pheasants on it. Several years later, I found one and bought it and gave it to Jerry to bring closure to the prank.

In the summer of 1978, I accepted my first administrative job in Waseca, Minnesota. A couple of weeks before we were moving to

Waseca, Dr. Cliff and Mary Helling asked us to go to dinner and a movie. Cliff was my boss and one of my mentors. We went out to dinner with them, and I said that we really didn't want to go to a movie. We could have a nice leisurely dinner and some friendly conversation. They agreed. Cliff and Mary picked us up in one of his old restored Fords. Cliff had a hobby of restoring old '33 Fords. Those cars are works of art.

The four of us had a nice dinner and conversation and Cliff was pushing us to go to some new movie. We didn't want to go to a movie and suggested that they take us home, and we could have a cup of coffee at our house. After some pouting by Cliff, they agreed to our plan. We were having dinner in New Hope and we lived in Maple Grove about six to seven miles away. My wife and I were riding in the back seat of this restored Ford; and when we pulled up to our house, there were lots of cars parked on the street. I saw someone peaking around the back corner of our house. We had a swimming pool in our back yard; and with all of the cars and seeing someone peaking from behind the house, I jumped to the conclusion that someone had drowned in our swimming pool. I immediately began to hyperventilate and Cliff was dragging me out of the car as I was gasping for air. I remember saying, "Someone has drowned in our pool."

Cliff, Mary, and my wife were all saying, "No, no, relax; it's a surprise going-away party for you." Then I began to focus on familiar faces that were coming out of the house and my regular breathing started to return.

The little beer, wine, and alcohol that we had in our house had been long ago consumed by the surprise party guests. After a short while, they had a gathering in our dining room and living room area. They proceeded to do some "roasting" of me. At one point, as I sat on a three-foot-high wooden stool, Jerry Davis walked up to me with a big banana-cream pie sitting on his open palm. Jerry said, "You know, Nathan, I never did get even with you for cutting the pheasant tie off me several years ago."

As I sat on that stool, I thought, *Jerry, you don't have the guts to mush that pie in my face.* At about that time, he moved in and stuck that pie full-force into my face. There was instant laughter and cheering. I managed to get some of the pie in my mouth, but I had pie up my nose, in my ears, and in my eyes. I was led to the sink, where after several rinses, I got most of the pie either off or out of my orifices. Then I went into the bathroom, did a quick shampoo, and went back to the party and to some great parting-gifts. Someone told me later that after Jerry had clobbered me with the pie that he had run and hidden behind a couch. If I know Jerry, he didn't do that move out of fear but rather to get the most out of his banana cream pie victory.

The Nineteen Eighties

Heart Transplant number 47

I have known few individuals in my life who possess the attributes of Dennis Deanovic. Dennis was an elementary principal at Jefferson Elementary School in Faribault, Minnesota, when I first met him in 1979. The best words that I have to describe Dennis are vibrant, enthusiastic, caring, loving, dedicated, bright, persistent, fair, knowledgeable, courageous, religious, hardworking, and a man with a laugh that is truly infectious. He is my friend.

Dennis had suffered a heart attack in his forties and the damage that he sustained had severely weakened his heart. In 1985 Dennis' heart had deteriorated to such an extent that he was hospitalized and his heart was functioning at less than fifteen percent. I've been told by cardiologists that the heart is probably the only organ that we have that functions normally at about sixty to seventy percent of its working capacity. According to the cardiologists that I've talked to, that's all of the effort that the heart needs to do in order to keep the body functions operating normally. Therefore, this muscle, about the size of your fist, is one mean functioning machine. When the heart functions at less than twenty percent, major problems occur, so I have been told.

Dennis's heart had all but given up functioning. He was on life support because his heart could not give his lungs enough oxygen, his kidneys enough power to function properly, his brain was lacking oxygen, and he was becoming jaundiced because his liver was not working well. As we know the language, "He was on his death bed."

As you might expect, his wife Liz was a bundle of nerves. The doctors at the University of Minnesota Hospitals had told Dennis that he would die without a heart transplant. Understand, that it was 1985 and his insurance company was declaring that heart transplant surgery was still experimental; therefore, they would not cover the expense. Liz had talked to the bankers and their lovely home, although paid for if sold, would not generate enough revenue to pay for the transplant surgery.

Dennis barely audible whispered to his son, "Dan, I desperately need your help or surely I will die."

Dan left the hospital room and drove back to Faribault, Minnesota, with tears streaming periodically down his face. He was anxious and felt the weight of the world on his shoulders. *What can I do? Where can I turn? Whom do I know?*

When Dan arrived at home he had laid out, what seemed to him, a foolproof plan. He was twenty-one years old and he had decided that there was no problem so big in this country that could not be solved by the President of the United States. He went into the house and dialed The White House.

The phone call at the White House was answered by an aide and Dan told him the story of his Dad's dilemma and how the insurance companies had been unwilling to participate in the surgical fees for his Dad's proposed transplant, and what was he to do. Dan said to the White House aide, "Can you help me?" He went on to tell the aide that this was not experimental surgery and that it had in-fact been performed all over the country. The White House aide recommended that he contact his congressman and gave him the name and number to do that. The aide also recommended that Dan call the Minnesota Attorney General and seek his help.

This Congressional aide called the attorney general in Minnesota and asked him to look into the Deanovic matter. The Minnesota Attorney General called Deanovic's insurance company. After a few short days, the insurance company reconsidered its position. When a suitable donor match was available, Dennis Deanovic did, in fact, receive a heart transplant. In the meantime Deanovic's other son Chris had given an emotional speech in his class at Bethlehem Academy in Faribault. For the record, according to the University of Minnesota Hospitals, Dennis Deanovic was the recipient of heart transplant number forty-seven.

Dennis had one of those spiritual out-of-body-experiences when he was on his way to the operating room for his surgery. I could never duplicate in writing that experience as told to me by Dennis. To see his facial expressions, hear his various speech inflections, and feel his emotions as he tells of that experience is beyond my writing skills. I can tell you this that I was moved to tears when he has shared that spiritual experience with me.

Dennis is still vibrantly alive at the time of this writing, twenty years after his transplant. Dennis and I have always laughed a lot together in person or on the phone, and I am always wound up like the bunny in the Energizer battery commercials after I talk with him.

Tyler Paul Johnson

Tyler Paul Johnson is our first grandson and he came to stay with us in Moorhead in 1988, when he was a little over two years old. Tyler was talking fluently at eighteen months and displaying an above-average vocabulary by the time he was two years old. He had not been away from his parents on an overnight stay in his first two years. This visit would be a first for Tyler as Jay and Tammy, his parents, were taking a short vacation.

My wife and I were somewhat apprehensive. What if he panicked because his mom and dad were gone hundreds of miles away? What would we be able to do if that occurred? How would we be able to comfort and to control those kinds of emotions if Tyler was upset? Sure we had adult children, but it had been some time since we had little children.

After several hugs and kisses from his mom and dad, they were finally ready to depart. We watched them leave our home and get into their car. Tyler was standing on a couch waving goodbye to them. What would happen when Jay and Tammy were no longer in sight?

As the car left our view, I wondered what the next move of Tyler's might be. Would he begin to cry uncontrollably? Would he throw a temper tantrum? The moment of concern would soon arrive.

As Tyler watched the car disappear, our anxiety level increased. When he could no longer see his parents' car, he turned around on the couch, looked us straight in the eyes, raised his right arm, and clenched his fist and proclaimed, "Let the good times begin." What a relief. What a relief.

A Stormy Boundary Waters Night

My dad, my brothers, and some other friends and relatives built a cabin for my parents when I was in the army in the summer of 1961. The cabin was located in the Minnesota Boundary Waters on Sand Point Lake, a stones throw from the Canadian border. The Minnesota Boundary Waters area consists of approximately one-million acres of magnificent wilderness land and water. The land abounds in white pine, birch, and aspen trees; some of them appear to be growing right out of the massive boulders that dot the lake's bays and islands. Mom and Dad had leased the land from the federal government for ninety-nine years. The feds, however, recanted and the last year that they had the property was 1987 when the land was returned to a wilderness area now known as the Voyagers National Park.

The cabin that they built on a solid boulder base was approximately 24' x 28'. The exterior siding had a log-cabin look with large front windows facing the east end the lake. There were two bedrooms in the back of the cabin and the front of the cabin was open and used for the kitchen, dining, and living room area. Believe me it was rustic. There was no running water so fresh water was hauled in containers from the main land for cooking and drinking.

There was an outhouse in back of the cabin about twenty-five feet away. My mother Florence had drawn cartoon characters on the inside outhouse walls and someone was always placing 'humorous" wall hangings in there. The cabin was only accessible by a boat ride of approximately thirty minutes from the main land. By 1961, Mom and Dad had been fishing up in that area for over twenty years, but the fishing would never be as great in the later years as it had been in the beginning.

Extra gas for the outboard motors had to be hauled from the main land, too. Over time my dad had installed a gas cooking stove and oven, as well as several gas lanterns inside the cabin. There were also a small gas heater and a gas-operated refrigerator. All of the appliances were powered by bottled gas, which was hauled to them by a vendor at the mainland at Crane Lake. My parents paid an annual fee to park their car and boat trailer at Hamburg's Resort on Crane Lake. Hamburg's did repair work on marine engines, sold fishing licenses, bait, groceries, gasoline, and fishing tackle in their store. If more groceries were needed, the small town of Orr, Minnesota, was no more than forty-five minutes by automobile.

When after forty-five years of employment my dad retired from the George A. Hormel meat packing plant, he and mom spent their entire summers at the cabin. Dad had built a very stable boat dock with his best friend Mel Finholt the summer before the cabin was built. Dad had also built a storage shed for fishing gear and a small refrigerator powered by bottled gas. Years later, he had added a solar-heated shower in the northwest corner of the shed. The shower reservoir was filled by starting a gasoline-powered pump that had a three-inch hose, which ran approximately fifty feet out into the lake. The solar-heated warm water did not last long, so to my knowledge, there was little singing done in that shower. One quickly learned to shower in late afternoons on bright sun-shiny days.

Dad had also rigged up an old washing machine to a one-horse-powered gasoline engine. The engine did not have a muffler so neighbors for a long ways knew when the Johnsons were doing their laundry. The distinctive sound of that engine bounding across the water was as discernable to the ear, as the old smoke signals in the sky were to the eye.

There was also a small wood-burning stove in the cabin that was stoked up for the cool mornings and evenings. The cabin had no insulation and only one storm door. Therefore, the last person to use the cabin in the fall would take any canned food that would expand if frozen. Expanded frozen food cans or broken soda-filled bottles would present an unnecessary mess in the spring. Winters were harsh in that part of the country. Dry soups and cereals, crackers, coffee, and the like were left in case someone was lost or had mechanical problems with their snowmobile and needed food and shelter. Dad only left a small padlock on the door because he figured that if someone wanted to break into the cabin, it would cause less damage that way. The cabin was never broken into during the twenty-five years that they had it.

There were curtains on the windows, a few chests with drawers, a dining room table with six chairs, one wash basin and mirror in the cabin and another similar wash basin set up on the porch outside, and a davenport with a hide-a-bed. Remember that all of the lumber to build the cabin and all of the furnishings had to be brought across the water by boat. That cabin was a cozy place and it got a lot of use. There were a number of books, games, and magazines for the rainy days.

My wife and I had been at the cabin the last few days of August, and we were going to drive home on the Sunday before Labor Day. We were to close the cabin up for the winter. Dad had also made solid wooden windows for the cabin so we had taken down the screens and stored them in the cabin. We had then installed the wooden windows, which would keep out any animals and the driving winter snows of Minnesota. We had installed all of the wooden windows except for one so that we would have some natural daylight in the morning. We had cleaned out the cupboards and packed the boat for the trip to the mainland in the morning. All that remained for us to do in the morning was to turn off the gas, tidy up the cabin, put on the last window, and put the small padlock on the door.

Rain had been threatening to happen all day and by seven that evening it was coming down in buckets. The wind was howling and there were periodic claps of thunder as the rain pelted the cabin. We were in bed sleeping by 9:30 p.m. My wife awoke me at a little after midnight and said there was someone at the door. I was startled and surprised because there were very few neighbors, and we had not seen any of them since we had arrived. I slipped on a shirt and some jeans as I heard someone yelling, "Mr. Johnson, we need help! Please come to the door." As I zipped up my pants, I thought, *Who are they and how do they know my name?*

The rain was still pounding the roof and sides of the cabin as I grabbed a flashlight and headed for the door. In the kitchen, I grabbed a stick match and lighted two of the globe gas lamps. As I approached the front door, I directed the beam of the flashlight through the window pane and could see several men peering in at me. They were absolutely soaked to the skin. I opened the door and invited them in. There were four of them. I said, "Who are you and what's going on?"

"I'm Father Frank O'Brian and these three men are seminarians. We got caught in this terrible storm in our canoes in the middle of the lake. Our canoes were swamped, but we stayed with them and kept our paddles until we washed up on the shore. We lost our tents, clothes, and all of our supplies. We've been stumbling along the shoreline for a couple of hours, but we couldn't find anyone home until we got here."

"How did you know my name?"

"There's a sign post at the end of your dock with the name Ted Johnson printed on it."

I had forgotten about that sign that someone had given to my dad as a gift. I had decided that their story sounded plausible; and even if it were untrue, they could most certainly overpower us, if that were their desire. My wife had gotten up, dressed, and came out into the kitchen area. She told them that we had very little left to eat since we were closing the cabin up for the season, but she would put something together for them to eat. In the meantime, I had taken them into my parents' bedroom and showed them boxes of dry clothes that were always on hand. They could change into dry clothes and get out of their wet ones. They were agreeable to that. The floor was cold so I put on some socks and shoes.

I started a fire in the wood stove and found a pound of bacon in our travel cooler, some luncheon meat, nearly a loaf of bread, butter, some pickles, and mayo. At the same time, my wife had begun to prepare some packaged chicken noodle soup and had brought out some saltine crackers. We also had a couple of cans of soda pop and four cans of beer left in our travel cooler. The men were famished and devoured all of the food and drink that we had prepared for them. They seemed like terrific young men and they were very polite. They had also taken time for prayer and had included us in their prayers. I told them that in the morning, we would take the boat and try to find their canoes. They said they had pulled their canoes onto the shoreline high enough where they shouldn't get washed back into the lake.

We pulled out the hide-a-bed for two of them and let the other two use my parents' bed. Needless to say, I didn't go back to sleep right away because I kept thinking, *What if they aren't who they say they are?*

When morning came, we put their semi-dry clothes in plastic garbage bags and prior to going down to the boat had a meager breakfast. The food was basically gone. We made Tang, an imitation orange juice, put peanut butter on crackers, and had some good hot coffee. The rain had ceased. The wind was still very strong and there were rows of white capped waves moving at us from across the lake. I would estimate the waves were between two and three feet high. Dad had a good eighteen-foot Lund boat and an eighty-horsepower Mercury motor at that time, which would have no problem handling the rough water.

The four men and I set off in the boat in the direction where they had walked the night before. Now, they could see the rough terrain that they had walked the night before in the dark stormy night. It took no more than fifteen minutes before we spotted the canoes and approached the shore line. It was uncharted water and I thought that I might ruin the prop on the motor and be disabled, so they jumped over the side of the boat with their garbage bags. The water was about waist deep, and they headed for their canoes with yells of thanks and good will. I slowly backed up the boat and headed back to the cabin. It took us less than an hour to finish up our chores at the cabin before we headed for Hamburg's at the mainland.

All along the way to Hamburg's, I expected to pass the two canoes. We never saw them, and I wondered if they had gotten swamped again. When we arrived at Hamburg's, I tied up the boat and headed up to the parking lot to get my car and Dad's boat trailer. As I walked through the store on my way to the parking lot, I grabbed a banana and there at the table eating breakfast were the four men. "Impossible," I said. "How did you guys get here so fast?"

Father O'Brian spoke, "The Lord was with us and we paddled really hard. The waves were so high that sometimes when we paddled all we got was air. We've loaded the canoes and we're heading for St. Paul as soon as we're done with breakfast."

For some reason, I said, "God bless you all."

Almost in unison they replied, "God bless you, too, Mr. and Mrs. Johnson."

There was once a clay pottery factory in Red Wing, Minnesota. Antique collectors have sought their products for decades. A few weeks after we were back home in Mankato, I went down to the post office to pick up a package. As I looked at the return address, I figured that it must have been from some relative of my wife's since I didn't recognize the name. When we opened up the package, it was from the four men who had swamped their canoes. It was a Red Wing Tea Pottery set, pattern known as "Bob White." No "teas" have ever been served in that set as I view it across the table from where I'm word processing this story. It is a very handsome pottery set and brings back memories of a stormy night in the Boundary Waters of Northern Minnesota.

The Nineteen Nineties

Posse Comitatus

I believe that the District Court Jury pools in Minnesota come about through a random selection of registered voters. As a person who voted nearly one hundred percent of the time in local, state, and national elections, I was surprised that I was not put into a jury pool until I was fifty years old. I served for one week on jury duty in Moorhead, Minnesota, which is a part of Clay County. I served during the course of that week on three jury-trials, and I was elected by my jury peers to serve as foreman twice; the third time, I refused to be considered for the election of foreman.

The subject matters for the three juries that I served on were assault, wrongful death, and theft. I will write a synopsis of the theft trial because it was rather strange.

I know very little about the extreme political groups in the United States; however, one of those political groups was known as the Posse Comitatus. The following quotation is taken from the Department of Justice, Federal Bureau of Investigation web site, "Posse Comitatus, also known as Sheriff's Posse Comitatus, is a loose knit, nationwide organization established in 1973. The group's objectives include resisting statutory authority related to federal, state, and local taxing authorities; and limiting the capability of federal, state, and local law enforcement officers; and limiting access of all law enforcement representatives in trespassing on individual property. The FBI conducted extremist white-hate investigations concerning the Posse Comitatus from 1972 through 1977. The organization was also investigated in 1980 through 1986 on possible domestic security/ terrorism activities."

A member of the Posse Comitatus political group was my first trial where I had the potential to sit on a jury. There was a jury pool of approximately twenty-five people and twelve would be selected to hear the case. We were called into the courtroom by the bailiff, one at a time. The purpose of that question and answer period was for each attorney to determine if a potential juror was prejudiced or might in fact be supportive of his position. The defense attorneys (and their clients) had our names, addresses, places of employment, and family status information, which seemed to me like too much information for someone to have about members of the jury.

For the jury selection process, I entered the courtroom and was asked to sit in the witness chair. The judge instructed me to answer the questions as honestly as I could. The next thing, as I recall, there was a man standing in front of me wearing a much too-small United States Air Force uniform as he could not button the front of the jacket. He looked to be about five-foot-six and had black hair combed down, which squared off on his forehead. He had a little black mustache just below his nose, shaped like Adolph Hitler's. I thought, *What the hell gives with this guy?*

He stood in front of me for perhaps one minute, which is a long time of silence in any setting, let alone a court of law. Finally, he spoke, "In the state capitol in St. Paul, which flag flies on top of the flag pole?"

"The United States flag," I responded.

"And, which flag flies below that flag?"

"The Minnesota state flag."

"That is all," the man in the air force uniform said.

The District Attorney said, "Please state your name."

"Nathan J. Johnson."

"Your address."

"One-eight-two-zero Twentieth Avenue South."

"Your occupation."

"President of Moorhead Technical College."

"I have no further questions, Your Honor," the District Attorney stated.

The judge responded, "You're dismissed for the present time, sir."

I went back to the jury room and waited. Those of us who had been called into the courtroom for questions were not only amazed at the brevity of the questions, but also the type of questions that were asked of us.

One other potential juror said about the man in the air force uniform, "He asked me to recite the Pledge of Allegiance to the Flag."

Another said, "He asked me to read the largest print on the face-side of a one-dollar bill."

Someone else said, "That guy's a nut case. He asked me if I wore red, white, and blue panties. The judge told him that he was out of order." She continued, "I told the judge I ain't gonna serve on no jury for this stupid ass. I think he's guilty as hell. The judge dismissed me from this case, see ya later," she said as she exited the jury selection waiting room.

We had determined in the jury room that the guy in the air force uniform was the one on trial and that he was defending himself. It took three hours for the jury to be selected and I was one of those selected. The judge directed the twelve of us and one alternate to meet and elect a foreman. I was elected foreman and the judge dismissed us for lunch, which was a boxed lunch brought into the jury meeting room.

The trial began at 1:30 p.m. that afternoon with the judge giving us directions.

The man on trial had borrowed a substantial amount of money from an area bank for new farm equipment and livestock. He didn't make any payments on his debt so the bank had gone with the sheriff to repossess his machinery, but it wasn't on his property. The man told them that a neighbor must have borrowed the machinery, but he didn't know which neighbor. The man sold the livestock and put that revenue in his bank savings account. The bank captured those assets in a flash as payment towards his unpaid loans. Not your smartest posse member.

The trial lasted for two days and the judge had much more patience with the man on trial than I could imagine. The man knew nothing of court room procedures and was always ranting and raving about his private property. The judge frequently warned him about his behavior; and by the second day, the judge had a man with a video camera recording every move of the man on trial.

The man on trial produced no credible witnesses. The attorney representing the bank did a fine job of presenting credible witnesses who gave believable testimony. When the jury went into deliberation, it was an initial chore for me to keep things under control. Twelve people silent for a couple of days had a lot to say, and they all wanted to talk at once. On that case, we deliberated less than one hour before we reached a verdict of guilty for the farmer in the tight air force uniform. I never did find out if he had served in the air force or had bought the uniform in a second-hand store.

I will tell you that spending that week with those jurors on three different cases renewed my faith in our judicial system. All of the jurors were sincere, cooperative, and thorough in the deliberation process. I was glad I was there and I was proud of the way that we conducted our business. Our jury system may not be perfect, but it's awfully darn good.

Lights Out

Cold winter winds whistled and carelessly trumpeted the icy driven BB-sized snow pellets against my office window. The weather was harsh evidence of the cold-reality of a winter morning in Minnesota. It was mid-morning, I had a fresh cup of coffee, and I was reading through my piles of daily mail.

My administrative assistant Jan had pre-determined what the most important pieces of mail were and stacked them in three priority piles on my desk. The three piles of mail were "Read and Act Today," "Get to it Soon," and "Read Sometime." Jan had attended a seminar a couple of years earlier and had come back with a great mail sorting idea. She used her best judgment as to what she discarded completely as "junk mail." That way I got access to the most important mail each day, without having to personally open and sort it. The only mail that she did not open was mail that appeared to be personal and addressed to me. I trusted her mail judgment, as well as her.

I tried not to read mail more than once, a tip that I had learned several years earlier in my administrative career at a time-management seminar. Sometimes, the lowest-priority pile of mail got quite large because of my busy schedule as a small college president. Since the nature of my job as a college president was to conduct or attend meetings both internally and externally, I tried to use my office time judiciously.

In 1988, I kept track of all of the meetings that I had attended that year, with agendas, both internally and externally and determined that I had attended nearly 800 meetings. I mention with agendas because it was my conviction that group meetings without agendas floundered from one topic to another and were a big waste of time. I

222222222222222

refused to attend those non-agenda meetings. In the 800 meetings that I attended that particular year, I did not count frequent daily formal or informal meetings that I had with one or two people. My job was to attend meetings, to meet with people, to create positive change, and to lead with a vision for the future. I felt good about my responses to problem situations, and I was frequently positively reinforced of my decision-making skills by union employees. Finding and implementing appropriate solutions to problems helped to sustain my administrative energy.

While reading my mail on that cold wintry and blustery day, all of a sudden the lights flickered briefly and went out. It was early morning and with the sunlight that was streaking through a frosty window pane, there was enough light for me to see. I was startled, but not yet concerned. My administrative assistant uttered a small expletive, which meant to me that she had lost much of her morning word processing work. She, like me, did not save her work as frequently as she should have. I sat in silence for perhaps 20 to 30 seconds thinking that it might just be a temporary power outage.

Then I got up from my chair, walked through my office door into the outer office, and noticed the darkened hallways. As I proceeded out into the hallway, I could hear the muddled concerns being voiced by staff and students. Then I spotted Moses Johnson, our head custodian, coming towards me down the hall. His nickname by staff members was Lefty (although most people on the staff called him Lefty, they probably thought he was so nick-named because he was "left-handed"). In fact, he was right-handed but had been born with two left feet, which was unknown to most people. Because he had been born that way, he had adjusted to it and had been labeled "Lefty," by some of his school mates, who had known of his misfortune. Moses wore custom-made shoes or boots and appeared to walk quite normally. Almost everyone called him "Lefty." I called him Moses.

Moses and I had frequent discussions about what it meant for a building to be "clean." How the two of us defined "clean" was never resolved. I prevailed in this matter, however, because I had personal experience in cleaning and supervision of building maintenance early in my career. Proper cleaning strategies were always a work-in-progress with Moses.

The power was out. There was Moses walking down the hall carrying a huge bolt-cutter, which he primarily used to cut locks off student lockers (Why students had lockers on a college campus I never did quite figure out). As Moses Johnson approached me, I said to him, "Hey Moses, what gives with the power outage?"

"I don't know, boss, I'm on my way to break a lock off this here woman's locker," as he gestured to an attractive young woman walking next to him.

"No you're not; we have over thirteen hundred students and employees in this building in the dark. We need to find out the cause of this power outage."

As he walked passed me he said, "It ain't no big deal. I'll look into it after I get the lock off of this here girl's locker."

By now he had gone about ten feet past me and I yelled, "Stop right now, the power outage is our number one priority; the lock can wait!"

Moses (muttered something which I could not distinguish, although I thought I detected the word prick, as part of it) gave me a disgusted look, went down another hallway, and I assumed to check on the power outage. I found out later that he had continued down that hallway and had taken the lock off the student's locker first, in spite of my explicit directions.

Furthermore, I discovered as I went to the East Side of the building that a construction crew working out on the street had accidentally cut our power source so we dismissed classes for the day. We could not operate without power, and it would take a few hours before the power would be restored.

I stayed at work and had enough window light in my office to resume reading my mail, and the heat was good for a couple of hours of work The power was restored by mid-afternoon; and by that time, I was the only one, other than the custodians, still in the building.

I had in the meantime written a letter of reprimand for Moses on my battery-powered laptop. It was my belief that Moses Johnson had failed to respond properly in an emergency situation. I could not believe that he could not recognize that the power outage was a higher priority than breaking the lock off of a student's locker. What had really ticked me off was that I had to tell him to react to the situation. In my mind, he had decided that he knew more about emergency situations than I did. I decided that his actions were a clear-cut-case of insubordination and wrote him a letter of reprimand.

I called ol' Moses on the inner-school phone before he left the building that day and told him that I wanted to see him the first thing in the morning because I would be giving him a letter of reprimand. I also called the area union representative and told him that I would be giving Moses a letter of reprimand the next day and that he was welcome to be present.

The next morning Moses and his union rep showed up, and I verbally explained what had happened the day before. I also had one of the college vice presidents present as a witness. I gave all of them a copy of the letter of reprimand and read it aloud. I told them that Moses had an opportunity to respond to the reprimand in writing and that if he did so that it would also be placed in his personal file. Moses did not say a word. The union rep said that I would probably hear from them again, and I felt confident that this issue was not over.

The custodians on our campus had a union dues membership and affiliation with a union organization in St. Paul, Minnesota, which was over two hundred and fifty miles way. About a week after the power outage incident, I received a call from a union steward in St. Paul; and we set up a meeting date to discuss the reprimand I had given Moses for two weeks later.

The appointed day came when I was to meet with Moses, the local union rep, and the St. Paul steward about Moses's reprimand.

Over the course of my career, I had been a labor union member, and a teachers' union "negotiation's man," as well as a member of the teachers' union for thirteen years. Those experiences, coupled with many college-graduate labor/management relations classes, personal incident involvement, contract negotiations, many management and labor seminars, and fifteen years of administrative practical experience, had adequately prepared me for that encounter.

I knew full-well that the union steward from St. Paul would come into my office and talk tough to impress his local union members and also send me a message that I should fear and respect "the brotherhood." I was familiar with the message since I had first heard the same kind of labor union message in the late 50s, as a construction worker.

Gathered in my office were Moses, the local union rep, the St. Paul union steward, and one of my vice presidents. I had coffee and cookies on hand to present a warm human relations environment. Everyone declined the coffee and cookies, but me.

Introductions were made and we had some small talk about the weather. I then reiterated why I had given Moses a reprimand. It was obvious to me that the St. Paul union steward, whose name was Bernard, would be their spokesman.

Bernard began slowly, like the little train chugging to get up the hill. He talked about what a fine employee Moses Johnson had been and how his record was clean, no other reprimands in his file. I thought, *Right, but the former administration wrote few letters of reprimand or letters of commendation.*

As Bernard droned on in his monotonous gravelly voice, he was getting louder and louder. Union steward Bernard was rapidly moving "the train up the hill" and trying to invoke management incompetence. Moses Johnson had a distinct look of pleasure on his face and was thoroughly enjoying Bernard's performance.

Bernard had just finished telling us that the punishment (the reprimand didn't fit the crime), when I interrupted him and said, "You know Bernard; I'm not hard of hearing."

Bernard didn't like the interruption and continued on with even more volume. I thought, *Enough of this,* and I interrupted him again, "A little less volume, please."

Bernard glared at me and was momentarily on a lower volume, but soon had resumed his case as the train was gaining momentum charging down the hill.

This time I jumped to my feet and slammed my fist on my desk and proclaimed, "All right, goddamn it, I've had enough of this bullshit; this meeting is over, now get the hell out of here." Coffee jumped out of my cup onto the desk top. There was immediate silence, and then they were all looking at Bernard. Bernard was busy writing on his tablet.

I was surprised that knowing what I knew about union and management relations, and the posturing that would probably take place, that this Bernard from St. Paul, had gotten to me. He had accomplished his mission. Almost always I was polite, well-mannered, and a good listener. Not, however, at that meeting.

Although my word choice was not the best, I certainly had their attention.

As they hurriedly exited my office, Bernard was writing on a notepad as fast as he could. I knew that I shouldn't have sworn at them, but he had made me angry. It was the worst language that I ever had used as a college president, but I found ways to rationalize for that atypical display of behavior. The vice president who was my witness wore a look of astonishment as he had never seen me act in such a manner. I apologized to him after the other three had gone.

Within thirty minutes, I got a call from the human resources manager who said that Bernard had stopped by and did not like the way he had been treated by me. I told the human resources manager my feelings about the meeting and that I expected to get a nasty letter from the St. Paul office representing the custodian. I never heard again from the local nor did I hear from Bernard. Moses Johnson never responded in writing to the written reprimand.

How Moses reacted to that power outage created an opportunity for change and I took advantage of it. Shortly thereafter, I created an administrative supervisory position for buildings and grounds and hired a new person. Moses retired when he was not hired for the new position.

Casey Falls for Me

Casey Robert Johnson is my youngest grandson and he was about one-and-a-half years old and was busy playing at our house in Moorhead, Minnesota. Casey jumped from a couch to a throw rug on a hardwood floor and the rug slipped and Casey crashed to the floor on his butt. I'm certain that it hurt and he began to cry instantly. I put out my arms and said, "Come to Grandpa Nate." He crossed the short distance with alligator tears rolling down his cheeks. I wrapped him in my arms and in an effort to cheer him up I pretended to peek inside the back of his pants and I exclaimed, "Oh, no Casey, you've cracked your butt!" The adults in the room laughed, but Casey cried louder as he was immediately concerned that he had broken his anatomy.

I gave him a big hug and told him that everything was okay and that I was just teasing him. Within a short time, he was back on the floor playing. I learned an important lesson about dealing with children's pain and self-esteem. Adult humor was beyond his comprehension and rightfully so. I'm sorry, Casey.

The Jailbird

I was attending a seminar for several days in San Diego; and the first morning, I decided to go outside for an early walk. It was early December and I was struck by the mild California weather, especially since I was only one day removed from the wind chill factor in Minnesota. As I exited the hotel, I was surprised to see heavy fog at 6 a.m. I would estimate that the temperature was probably in the high fifties and I was comfortably dressed in an athletic warm-up suit. It had been seven years on a New Year's Eve, at forty-five years old, that I had experienced a heart attack. I had tried to walk a couple of miles at least five days each week to stimulate my cardio-vascular system, and I had been smoke-free since the attack.

I had walked for approximately ten minutes when all of a sudden there was someone walking next to me. I was startled, but I tried to remain calm and said, "Good morning, how are you doing to day?" As I glanced to my right when giving the greeting, I could see an African-American man no further than two feet away walking stride for stride with me. He was wearing a black watchman's knitted cap, jean jacket, jeans, and black shoes. He was about the same height as me.

He responded, "Hey man, things ain't bad, but I need a favor."

"What kind of favor?"

"I need three dollars for bus fare to the state prison headquarters so I can get my cash."

"What cash?" We continued walking stride for stride in the early morning fog.

"I have 384 dollars coming for nine years of prison labor."

"You've been in prison nine years?"

"Yah, I just got released last night and I'm in need of bus fare."

"I don't carry any money when I'm walking; my money clip is back at the hotel."

(I was lying; my money clip with over a hundred dollars in cash was in my left front pocket.) "So why were you in prison?" as we continued to walk stride for stride.

"Manslaughter."

"Manslaughter? What did you do?"

"I killed a guy who raped my sister."

Oh, my god, I'm walking next to a guy in foggy San Diego, with plenty of cash and credit cards in my pocket, who has murdered somebody. "How do I know that you're telling me the truth?"

"I've got a pay invoice in my pocket so I can collect my pay at headquarters. Here you can take a look." He handed me a folded piece of paper that I couldn't read because my glasses were back in my room. We had been walking together for about ten minutes when I spotted a parked police car. I prayed that a police officer would be inside the car.

I said, "Well now, there's a police car; let's take this piece of paper over to him and have him read it to us."

"Okay," the ex-con said.

We walked over to the police car and I gently tapped on the driver's window. The officer looked annoyingly at me and rolled down his window. I said to the officer, "Would you please read this paper and tell me what it says. I've left my eye glasses back in my hotel room."

The cop took the paper, unfolded it, and rolled up his window. Then he turned on his interior lights and appeared to be reading the paper. When he was done, he rolled down the window and said, "He can collect 384 dollars for his work in prison."

"See, I was telling the truth," the ex-con said as the cop handed the paper back to me and rolled his window back up.

My first thought was *Hey, I could be in a life-threatening situation, and you roll your window back up. What a prick.*

I looked at the jailbird and said, "Well, I guess that you are right, but you'll have to walk back to the hotel with me so I can get some money for your bus fare."

"That-be cool, man." he said as we took off in the direction of the hotel.

"So what happened to your sister?" I asked after we had walked about a block. I was still nervous about my walking partner and I thought, *What a stupid goddamned question! Did I really want to stir this guy up?*

"She thought this guy was a friend who had dropped out of high school and she was helping him study for a GED test to get an equivalency high school diploma. The next thing she knew he was all over her and raped her. She was afraid to call the cops, but she called me. I went over to his apartment and waited in the shadows until he came home about 3 a.m. I hit him with a piece of pipe that I found in the alley and then I worked him over so he would never rape another girl."

"Do you feel bad about killing that guy?"

"Ya, I feel bad," he said. "I'm sorry I got caught."

Holy balls, I thought, here I am walking with a convicted murderer on a foggy morning in San Diego, no visible police support, and the guy feels no remorse for killing a guy.

Dawn was approaching, but the fog lingered on as I had picked up the walking pace. There were a couple of times when I thought that I would discreetly reach into my pocket, grab my money clip and just covertly toss it to my left into a vacant lot. I decided against that for fear of being seen by the jailbird.

As we continued walking, I could vaguely see the parking lot of the hotel and I began to feel safe. I said, "Are you hungry?"

"Yah, man, I ain't had nothin' to eat for twelve hours."

"I'm going to take you into this hotel and give you the finest buffet breakfast that you've ever had."

"You some kinda dude, man."

I was never more relieved in my life than when we walked into that hotel lobby and headed for the dining room. We were ushered to a table by a somewhat snooty hostess who asked me to produce my hotel key for identification. She looked at my guest and raised one eyebrow, a gesture open for interpretation; but I gathered that she was not going to slip Richard her phone number. When the waitress came, I told her that we wanted the breakfast buffet and that I wanted it charged to my room. She told us to help ourselves, but if we went back for seconds to be sure to use clean plates, I thought *Do we really look that bad?*

The ex-con's first name was Richard, but he said everyone in prison called him "Big Dick." I decided that I would call him Richard. It was obvious to me that he had never been to such a fine array of food displayed in his life. I showed him how to serve himself and we made our way back to our table. Poor Richard was famished for food, which had to have been an epicurean delight from prison grub. He ate a half plate of scrambled eggs, a large portion of hash brown potatoes, five sausage links, four slices of toast with preserves, a glass of milk, and a glass of juice before he went back for second helpings. My appetite wasn't so hot so I had some French toast and coffee.

On his second trip, Richard came back to the table with three pancakes smothered in butter and syrup and a half-dozen slices of bacon. I asked him if he wanted some coffee and he said he would prefer Coke, which I managed to get for him from a reluctant waitress.

By the time I was through with my fourth cup of coffee, and Richard was on his second Coke, he had easily eaten enough food for four people, belched out loud three times, but had not as yet farted out loud. Nobody chose to sit close to us. He looked at me with a big toothy grin; one of his front teeth was all gold, and said, "Man, this is the best meal that I've ever had in my life, and I want to do somethin' special for you."

"I'm glad you enjoyed your food, but I want nothing special from you."

"No man, you don't understand you're my guardian angel 'cause nobody has ever treated me like this. Let's go up to your room and I'll shine your shoes."

"No Richard, I don't need my shoes shined and here's the three bucks that you need for bus fare," (when he had gone back for seconds, I had peeled some ones from my money clip).

"Oh man, you are somethin' else. How am I ever going to repay you? Let's go to your room and I'll lick your body from one end to the other!"

I shuttered and I could feel the hair standing up on the back of my neck. *Did this mad-man think that I would actually take him to my room and let him do anything to me?* I had goose-bumps on my forearms, caused by fear, as I said to him, "Richard, I want nothing from you. Take the three bucks and get a bus down to prison headquarters so you can get your pay. The best way that you can repay me is for you to someday do something for someone less fortunate than you. That's it. I need to go to my room and get ready for a seminar that I am attending, but I want you to get up and leave first."

"No man, I gotta do somethin' for you."

"No, no, you can't," I said.

Richard the convicted murderer looked at me with glassy eyes and said, "I love you, man; even though I don't understand you. You are some piece of work, man."

We shook hands and Richard walked out of the hotel. I signed the guest check and headed back to my room for a shower. I didn't walk again the rest of that week in San Diego.

Usability Systems, Inc.

My brother David worked for over twenty-five years for International Business Machines (IBM) starting out as a Customer Engineer, then teaching others to be Customer Engineers; but most of his time was spent in sales and marketing IBM main-frame computers in Georgia and Louisiana. He played a key role in providing IBM and its customers with valuable user input through usability evaluation of products and processes. His experience with usability evaluations at IBM deepened his conviction that the usability process had applicability in virtually every business.

David took an early retirement from IBM at age 49; and along with a partner, created Usability Systems, Inc. a turnkey solution to organizations that needed help in creating their own usability programs. After a few years, David bought out his partner and became the sole proprietor. To my knowledge, he never employed more than five to ten people because that was all the employees that were needed. At one time he employed his sons Bruce, Reed, and Tim, as well as siblings Darlene and Ray (a retired IBM manager) and Ray's wife, Carol. David's wife Helen was also an integral part of the new company, and she was also employed in management with IBM. The easiest way for me to describe his business is to quote from the company's present web site.

I quote, with permission, from the Usability Systems, Inc. website:*

Usability Systems, Inc. (USI) began as a family business in 1987 and grew out of David Johnson's heartfelt conviction that we all benefit from products that are easy to use. Although the principal of this statement seems simple in theory, everyone knows that a product's ease-of-use becomes apparent only when it is not easy to use. Ease-of-use does not simply appear in products; it must be developed, researched, and implemented. USI is committed to providing the processes and tools that enable vital input to be gathered from the target audience of virtually any product.

While our company has seen the emergence of many great technologies over the past sixteen years, we continue to believe the best way to ensure a product will have usable characteristics and provide an enjoyable experience is to incorporate input from the people for whom the product is created.

We also believe that user experience research should not be regarded as a procedure used only by development teams but rather as a procedure that encompasses every aspect of product creation. This multi-level procedure is exemplified through the direct correlation between user input and the resulting customer satisfaction and profit. Ultimately, everyone wins when a company appreciates, supports, and incorporates the needs and opinions of their clientele.

USI offers expertise in many areas, but our greatest asset is that we continue to uphold the passionate belief that our company was founded upon. User input affects every aspect of a product and company. We look forward to the opportunity to work with and for you. Allow us to ensure that your product will meet the expectations of its users!
*www.UsabilitySystems.com

Said another way, one of the initial ways that USI began working with major United States companies was to install laboratories at their corporate training sites. For training purposes, new or existing employees would be asked to assemble a product that was going to be sold. Supervisors could watch the product being assembled from a vantage point that would not interfere with the employee doing the assembly and would permit the managers to discuss what they were viewing without the knowledge of the assembler. The USI system was developed with the use of closed circuit audio and visual state-of-the-art technology. The training session could also be video taped for later discussion.

The people doing the assembly would be "typical" employees not people with high levels of mechanical skills. The purpose of the training exercise was to see just how easy it was for the employee (consumer) to unpack the product and follow the directions provided for the assembly of the product. Watching product assembly ease or difficulty might be a contributing factor in determining whether a retailer wanted to carry the product line or not. Similar type labs were set up at manufacturing facilities to improve quality control. This is my understanding of how the company began and many of its processes are much more sophisticated and complex today.

I'm told by my nephews that their dad never missed an opportunity to sell the benefits of usability. He was often found selling to a salesperson that had called upon him for his business. When a salesperson came by the office to solicit business, David would let them finish their presentation and then turn the table and tell the salesperson about his usability evaluation process. Then he would give a short tour of the usability lab and point out to the salesperson how his usability system could benefit the salesperson's company. David was always promoting.

Sometime in 1993 my brother David developed cancer and in the fall of 1994 his son Bruce sent out the following letter:

The Wild Ducks...Flocking together to soar to new heights.

Dear Friend,

We need your help. More importantly our dad, Dave Johnson, needs your help! And never before could you provide so much help with so little effort.

As you may know, Dad went through an autologous bone marrow transplant in July. Recovery was steady through mid-September, when he began to feel weak. Last week we found out that the lymphoma has come back. Well, this time we're going to will this cancer away through a drug called Fludarabine (flu-dar-a-been), which is still in the test stages at the National Cancer Institute. Now, to make sure this drug does its job, we need to enlist your services.

Many of you are already providing a tremendous amount of love and support. Now we just want to organize and channel that input to

161

exponentially increase its effectiveness. Recently, we read an inspiring book that helped us see how we can give a little back to the man that has virtually formed our lives. The book is Where the Buffaloes Roam by Bob Stone. In this book, Bob talks about the formation of a team of his friends and relatives (the Buffaloes) to help him fight his cancer. If you want to read this book, give us a call. We purchased a few and would gladly send you one.

To help Dad in his fight, we are forming a team of our own — the Wild Ducks. The goal of this newly formed flock is to generate positive energy and prayerful petition to help him win this battle. Won't it be great to look back on this a year from now and reflect on the power of team, the power of prayer, and the power of God.

Here's what we need you to do:

Write a letter. In your letter, please recall a memory and an inspiration that you would like to share with Dad. If you don't know Dad directly, but know of him through someone who does, write something about that connection. The letter (or card) can be any length. Be creative and make some reference to being a member of the Wild Ducks.

Say a prayer asking for Dad's healing every morning at 8. If you are around other Wild Duck members, join together. We will all be in the moment together, and Dad is sure to feel the warmth.

Pass this letter on to at least one other person that you know Dad has touched. We would like to see the team reach 500 members by November.

We sincerely hope that you will join the Wild Ducks in our mission to call on God's power to heal our Dad. We look forward to hearing from you and hope that you will help us grow the flock.

Sincerely,

The Wild Ducks
Mail your letter to:
Dave Johnson
C/o The Wild Ducks
1150 Alpha Dr. Suite 100
Alpharetta, GA 30201

The formation of the Mighty Ducks was a wonderful idea and provided great inspiration for my brother David and his family. Unfortunately, it was not enough as David passed away in December, 1994 at the age of fifty-seven. When we went to Georgia for his funeral, I remember that the walls of their dining room were covered with letters and cards from "Mighty Ducks" well-wishers. As a matter of fact, I used some of the writing on those walls as part of the eulogy that I gave at David's funeral. I learned a great deal from reading those letters of inspiration to my brother and his family. The twenty years preceding David's death, we seldom saw each other more than once or twice a year, although we talked more frequently on the phone. He was living in Georgia and I was living in Minnesota.

I had never known what a humanitarian David had been, nor did I know how long he had been working with the homeless in the Atlanta area until he died. He was one of my mentors and I really love and miss him. If he were alive today, he would be so proud to see and know of his four sons, daughter, their families, and his wife Helen's accomplishments. They are all greatly talented people and I believe that David had a major influence on their lives.

Before David's death, he saw his vision realized to a large extent through the widespread acceptance of usability by companies, universities, and governments around the world.

Do You Know Who I Am?

I was visiting a friend in a rest home and as I was leaving the building there was a pleasant looking resident sitting in a chair who smiled at me.

I smiled back and said, "Good morning and I hope that you have a great day."

She responded, "Good morning and you have a great day too."

I was a little surprised at her rapid response to my greeting and gushed, "Do you know who I am?"

"No, but if you stop at the front desk, they will tell you."

The Green Plaid Skirt

Ambling down the hall, the potential new student appeared to be about six-foot-five, trim with wide shoulders and was by himself. I guessed him to be in his mid-twenties. His hair was blondish-brown and was mostly concealed underneath the brim of a tan cowboy hat. Jutting up from the brown hatband was a turquoise feather, probably reluctantly given up by some proud peacock. He had on a chestnut-colored leather sports jacket and a lime green tee shirt. In a kind of contemporary way, he had about a week's growth of beard stubble. *Nice western outfit, so far,* I thought. What surprised me the most were not his metal-toed brown cowboy boots, but the mid-knee green plaid skirt that went swish-swish as he moseyed down the hall way. This guy was not your typical Scottish Highlander parade regalia or some Hollywood off-set Roman Centurion.

Previously, my secretary had slipped into my office and whispered to me, "Come and see her."

"See whom?"

"I just got a call from admissions and a potential new student is coming down the hall."

"Why should I be concerned about this particular new student?"

"You'll see," she had said, with a twinkle in her eye.

I had reluctantly risen from behind my desk and walked out of my office into the administrative reception area, which had floor-to-ceiling windows. I had positioned myself behind a huge green plant, and I sheepishly felt like Inspector Closeau, from the *Pink Panther* movie series.

"Holy balls," was my first verbal reaction (not a real astute college president proclamation).

I had looked at my secretary, who was looking back at me and I asked, "What gives?"

"I think he's some kind of pervert; you better talk to someone in Admissions."

This man was going to create unexpected decisions for an experienced leader. As a Midwestern small college president, I can tell you that there are not any college courses or management seminars that will prepare you for decisions like the one involving the green plaid skirt.

I went back to my office to resume work on the college budget. Getting on task was difficult at first. I kept having those green plaid skirt flashbacks. Anyway, I had more numbers to crunch. Let one of the vice presidents worry about some cowboy walking the halls in a green plaid skirt.

A short time later, two staff secretaries in their mid-thirties knocked gently on my door and asked to speak with me. They were normally shy, but now appeared to be exasperated. They told me that the potential new student that I had seen walking down the hall earlier that day was going to have a sex change. I believe to be politically correct it would be referred to as a "trans-sexual gender manipulation." (In situations like this guy, apparently, the mind feels that the gender is not the same as the physical properties; therefore, he wants to make the appropriate change.)

In the previous week an old army buddy from Missouri had sent me the following email:

After a long night of love making this guy rolls over, was looking around when he noticed a framed picture of another man on the night stand by the bed. Naturally, the guy begins to worry. "Is this your husband?" he inquired nervously.

"No, silly," she replied, snuggling up to him.

"Your boyfriend then?" he asked.

"No, not at all" she said, nibbling on his ear.

"Well, who is he then?" demanded the bewildered guy.

She calmly replied, "That's me before the surgery."

The two secretaries continued. Furthermore, this potential new student has to gender role-play for a year before the operation would be performed. And, what was I going to do about "This Man" role-playing in the women's restroom. Why, according to them, he was tall enough to peer over the privacy toilet-stall walls. That was true.

I slipped into semi-consciousness and I visualized this man standing normally, skirt up and peeing into the toilet, splashing little water droplets on his shiny boots. Then in my mind's-eye I saw "Tex," with this huge Stetson hat, peering over the stall at the woman sitting next door. My final vision saw him sitting on the throne and applying eyeliner as he held a small mirror in his callused hand. In this brief interlude of escape, I was interrupted by one of the two secretaries who were inquiring about my proposed action, concerning this grave matter.

I thanked them for stopping in and I told them that to my knowledge, he had not as yet enrolled at our college and not to worry about something that had not become a reality. By mid-afternoon, the head of the college secretaries' union had approached me and requested a group meeting for four o'clock that day to resolve this pending dilemma of the green plaid skirt.

The room was buzzing with twenty-plus secretaries, when I walked promptly into the room at 4 p.m. Someone had ordered cookies and coffee, and I wondered silently if we would be there until six. I had been president several years by then, and I normally looked forward to my monthly meetings with the secretaries. They were a wonderfully talented group of people with a great flare for creativity when we had social functions. And, I was always amazed by their direct approach to questioning or offering of suggestions for the solutions to college issues. They were more open and honest than the teaching staff. From the beginning, I had reinforced the support staff's candid approach to problem solving.

The union president sent the first volley, "We're not going to enroll this queer are we?" (I winced at the derogatory description and thought she needs Human Relations 101.)

A financial aid secretary queried, "Isn't it true that they threw this guy out of the Moorhead State University?"

The extension secretary quickly said, "I'm not going in any restroom with some male pervert hanging out or peering over the stall wall at me!"

"I'll call the attorney general," another stated.

One secretary just audibly stated, "I think women students will drop out if you permit this to happen."

One rather matronly secretary, who always worked on her knitting during our meetings, huffed, "I'll give that cowboy a sex change that he won't soon forget," as she held up one of her knitting needles.

In reply to that, someone else said, "You go girl." This caused the group to laugh and I waited for the room to calm down.

Those kinds of comments went on for about ten to fifteen minutes until the statements were beginning to be repetitive. I thought it was time to intervene since most of the women had had ample opportunity to ventilate their frustrations.

My first posit to them was that I would not tolerate the use of prejudiced language terms like "queer" and "pervert," and the like to describe people with different life styles from our own.

"Furthermore, not to treat this individual as an equal would be discriminatory," I reasoned.

What I told that anxious gathering of secretaries that afternoon was that if the "new student" enrolled that he could use the small restroom next to my office until the surgery had been completed. When my office area had been constructed, they had built a small rest room right next to it. I presumed for presidential pontificating. I seldom used it; primarily, the administrative secretaries used that facility.

This approach seemed acceptable to many of those assembled, but body language told a different story, arms folded across their chests and wrinkled brows. I told them that once he became a student, I would give him explicit instructions on what restroom facilities were available to him and the consequences for not following my directive. I was also concerned about what potential conflict would occur if he walked into the men's restrooms in his green plaid skirt. Then, I told them, "After the surgery has been performed, 'she' will be permitted to use any of the women's public restrooms on campus. It would be her right."

That particular meeting had run its course and it was time to exit stage left. I grabbed a couple chocolate-chip cookies and a hot cup of coffee and walked back to my office thinking for an old guy, I had handled that situation about right. "Gender manipulation, what's next?" I secretly wished that the man in the green plaid skirt would not enroll. It had the potential for more legal wrangling, and legal matters seemed to take up more and more of my time.

I had just downed the cookies and was finishing up my coffee when Richard the VP from student services stuck his head in my door and asked the customary, "Have you got a minute?"

The thing about Richard was that he could never accomplish anything in a minute. I'd bet that if he had ever played the minute waltz on his piano, it would have lasted seven to eight minutes. I invited Richard into my office.

Nervous Richard was another one of the vice presidents that I had inherited when I took the job several years earlier. When Richard was nervous, he had a way of sitting in a chair and squirming as if he were trying to get out of a straight jacket. Administrative decisions were really hard for him, and he avoided them whenever he could. Worse than his administrative decision-making skills, however, was his attire. That day he had on a red and blue-on-white striped shirt, a yellow tie with colored balloons on it, a dark brown sports jacket, and gray and blue checkered pants. I kid you not. He was the only guy I have ever known who mixed so many different types and colors of fabric so poorly. I always sat next to him at administrative meetings so his apparel wouldn't distract me. The staff, behind his back, called him "Polyester-Rich."

I overlooked his clothing choices. I had worked a lot with Richard to improve his administrative decision-making skills and his adversity to conflict resolution. The most endearing quality about Richard, however, was that he had a heart of gold and would do anything to help any student. He may have looked like a lump of coal but he was a diamond of a gem with his student and staff relationships. He had a knack for seeing through liars and phonies. He could get to the root of a student's problem more quickly than anyone I had ever known. I had been trying to transfer those student problem-solving skills into the administrative arena, and he had been showing some improvement. The road to heaven is paved by the Richards of the world.

I asked Richard what his secretaries had to say about the brief meeting that I had just conducted. He said his secretaries had mixed emotions after returning from the meeting about the cowboy and were still worried about their privacy. Many times I thought, Richard sided more with the employees than the administration, especially with difficult decisions, but he was always honest with me. I trusted Richard.

"I just helped Toni fill out an enrollment application and dropped him off at the financial aid office on my way down here," Richard stated.

I inquired, "Was Toni the cowboy in the skirt?"

"That's the one," said Richard. "His first name on his high school transcript was Antonio," stated Richard, "and he wants to be treated like a woman."

"So I've heard, and we'll all do our best to accommodate him," I responded.

I asked Richard to go back and wait for Toni to exit the financial aid office and bring him to my office. With Richard present, I would then give him my explicit restroom decree.

Richard squirmed some and said, "Sure thing, boss." He had a smirk on his face as he walked out of my office on the way to lasso Toni when he exited the financial aids office.

I thought how much had changed in the past twenty years since I had first become an administrator, and specifically what had happened during that particular work day. I thought about one of my mentors, Dr. Ben Trochlil, who after decades of public school administration would typically say,

"Isn't it great? Every day we come to work and it's different. We have different opportunities to resolve conflict, solve problems, and create learning at all levels. Isn't it great?"

Although Toni never did enroll at our college, he caused a fair amount of stress for many of us.

The Twenty-First Century

The Roots Search Began

Amsterdam, Holland

In the autumn of 1999, twelve people began meeting and discussing a trip to Europe in search of the roots of the Speikers family located primarily in southern Minnesota. Ed Speiker from the Minneapolis area was the driving force behind the initial gathering. You may have noticed that Ed Speiker had no "s" in his name and that was not a typographical error. Apparently, one of Ed's ancestors owned a repair shop and had a sign painted with his name on the side of the building. The painter either did not know how to spell Speikers or had run out of space for the "s." Thus, their family name became Speiker as a result of a sign painter's error.

Six of us were closely related and six of us were related at some distance. The three Speikers (Spy-kurs) daughters of Ferdinand and Lucy Speikers and their husbands, Mary Lou and Charlie Jirik, Joanne and Jim Dalglish, and Charlotte and Nathan Johnson were six of the traveling companions. In the September of 2000, shortly after I had retired, the twelve of us flew to Amsterdam, Holland. Although, the two groups of six started out together in Amsterdam, our itineraries were somewhat different after we left Holland.

Charlotte and I had a flight that arrived in Amsterdam a few hours after the others in our group. We connected up with our immediate relatives at the Schipol International Airport in the Netherlands, gathered our luggage, and took an airport shuttle to our car rental agency. Jim Dalglish had made the vehicle reservations and the three guys had all gotten international drivers licenses, which you can get without a written or behind-the-wheel-test. Upon arrival, we found out that they were not needed.

At the car rental agency, we gave them our passports and drivers' licenses for verification and they brought around the 2000 Volvo van that Jim had requested. We checked the vehicle over for nicks and dents and had the attendant record them on the rental agreement, so that we wouldn't be assessed a fee for damages when we returned the vehicle. I asked the attendant if there were any specific rules that we should know about driving in Amsterdam and Europe in general and he said,

"Just use your common sense, drive politely and defensively, and never pass on the right."

It was good advice.

The white van had bucket seats in front with two rows of bench seats behind and enough storage space behind the second bench seat to store our entire luggage. Each of us had at least one large suit case and some also had smaller ones. It was a much larger van than I was used to seeing in the United States. We loaded up our luggage and I was the first designated driver. When I jumped up into the driver's seat, I was somewhat surprised to see a manual floor stick-shift and I hadn't driven something like that for many years. There were four forward gears and one reverse. It took a little while to get comfortable with where the four forward speeds were located in the shifting pattern and at what speeds to be driving in each gear. I have often equated driving skills with athleticism, and I have always fancied myself as a good safety-conscious driver. My record speaks for itself since I have had only one moving traffic violation, which occurred when I was seventeen.

I have to admit that I wasn't prepared for the traffic that we would encounter in that first hour of driving in Amsterdam. When we got into the city, I had never seen so many bicycle riders in my life. The streets were narrow. There were thousands of both motorized and non-motorized bikes, cars, buses, electric powered street cars, and pedestrians. We were also trying to figure out the traffic signs and signals.

"How come so many bikes?" The answer, "There is hardly anywhere to park a car!"

There were bicycles chained together, chained to bike racks, lamp posts, and trees, and some had removed the front wheel and taken it with them. One of my first observations was that the city was full of young people and all age groups appeared to be much leaner than your typical Americans. Diet, exercise, and heredity must be the correct formula for staying slim in Holland. Both walkers and bicycle riders moved at a fast pace.

Although each of us men in our group took turns either driving or reading the map for directions during our trip, I was better at driving than navigating a map. Jim seemed to be the best map reader and Charlie Jirik seemed okay doing either task.

Charlie Jirik was a retired grocer and his wife Mary Lou is a retired public health registered nurse/supervisor in Carver County, Minnesota. Mary Lou lives on the old Speikers' family farm in Watertown, Minnesota. Charlie, a victim of cancer, passed away in January 2004. When you hear people talk about the "Good Guys in Life," Charlie goes right to the top of the list. Charlie's yard, home, and the remaining farm buildings are immaculate. As a matter of fact, Charlie had a group of volunteer grounds workers at the Immaculate Conception Catholic Church in Watertown known as "Charlie's Angels." Mary Lou is a piano teacher, church organist, Master Gardner and has the flower and vegetable gardens to prove it. The home, yard, and gardens could easily be the cover photo on any home and garden magazine.

Jim Dalglish is a retired Northern States Power executive and his wife Joanne is a retired registered pediatrics nurse and they reside in Grand Forks, North Dakota for part of the year, Sierra Vista, Arizona for the winter, and Bemidji, Minnesota for the summer. Jim supervised the North and South Dakota Northern States Power operation for nearly two decades. Jim and Joanne are some of the most ardent University of North Dakota fans that you will ever know, especially when it comes to ice hockey. Jim is an amateur poet, song writer, and guitar player specializing in cowboy lyrics. Joanne is the organizer, planner, and keeper of the social calendar for that dynamic duo.

My wife Charlotte is a retired college business education teacher, and I am a retired college/school administrative leader. Charlotte has held state collegiate leadership education positions in Minnesota, held a governor's appointment to a mid-western higher education commission for several years, and is a catalyst for community volunteer activities. She wrote and published a book in June, 2004 on the history of Glenville, Minnesota. With the six of us in that van for over half a month, there was never a lull in the conversation.

As I was maneuvering our way through Amsterdam in search of our hotel, I came to a stop behind a street crew in a dump-truck. The truck stopped. The men got out. They then proceeded to put up a barrier right behind their truck and in front of our van. It was a two-way street. There was traffic at our bumper behind us that began blowing their horns, and I could not go forward. It was a simple decision. I turned the wheel hard to the right and gently drove up over the curb. I proceeded slowly down the sidewalk for perhaps one hundred feet, and then I drove back onto the street. I nervously watched in the rearview mirrors for a traffic cop to appear, but all I heard were the cheers from my traveling buddies.

When we arrived at our destination, the Tulip Inn, there was no parking on the street and we had to ask the hotel personnel where we could park. They showed us where the single garage door was for the hotel. We had to wait several minutes for the single lane one-way traffic to stop so that we could approach the garage and maneuver the van back and forth so that we could drive into the opening. They opened up a garage door that went underground, and I slowly drove down into the bowels of that hotel. It took some time going backwards and forwards before I could fit that van into one of those small interior parking spaces. After parking the van, I felt good. I had not run over anyone or anything. We had arrived.

After the six of us had checked into the hotel, we went for a leisurely walk. At one time or another, each of us was nearly hit by a speeding bicycle on the sidewalk. Although the sidewalks were probably ten to fifteen feet wide, there was a continuous white line painted about three feet from the curb. Those three feet were reserved for the bicycles and small motorized bikes as well. When we were walking and heard a "ka-ching, ka-ching," the sound of a bicycle bell being activated on the handlebars, the person who had ventured into the sidewalk bicycle lane would quickly get out of the way. Although we had some close encounters, the worst thing that happened to us was a glaring look from the passing bicyclist.

The next morning, we had a wonderful European buffet breakfast that was included in our stay. There was a nice assortment of fresh fruit, cold meats and cheeses, bread and hard rolls, fruit preserves, hard-boiled eggs, cold and hot cereals, scrambled eggs and sausage links, juice, and good rich coffee.

We left the Tulip Inn for the day to go to a large public library in downtown Amsterdam where we would meet up with our other six traveling friends. We did spend some time looking for a parking place and then we went into a bank to use an ATM machine to get some more Euros, the European money used in several countries. As we knew from previous travels, the exchange rate was always the best from ATMs. My wife, it seemed to me, was more concerned about the security of her travelers checks and passport than I was. She kept her travelers checks hidden in a small money bag stashed inside her bra. My guess is that it was not only hard to get at when she wanted to get cash, but also quite uncomfortable.

Prior to our trip, the Speikers' sisters had thought their father's ancestors had come from Germany, but Ed Speiker had thought they had come from Holland. After our brief trip to the bank, we walked over and found the other six travelers in the Amsterdam library. There happened to be an amateur genealogy group in the research section of the library and they were very accommodating for our group. They knew their way around the library and that day they began an earnest search for the Speikers of old. After just a few hours of research, the group had discovered the ancestral trail and it led to a church in a small town not too distant. I'm not certain that we would have been able to find the information in the time that we had allotted for Amsterdam if it had not been for those extremely helpful genealogists. We gave them a donation for their organization and thanked them profusely.

We went to the Speikers ancestral town and found the church with the help of a gas station attendant. People were so polite and helpful to us. The church was locked and closed, but we found a receptionist in the parsonage that let us inside the church and gave us a tour. The church had the baptismal records that would reflect the work of the genealogists. The Speikers were indeed from Holland and not Germany. I have never been quite certain if that was welcomed news by the three sisters. Charlotte seems to think that she has some Jewish lineage, although she has no specific historical data that can back up that notion.

The last night in Amsterdam after dinner the other foursome in our group went for a walk down into a "red-light" prostitution area, which was not far from our hotel. They later told of live mannequins in store-front windows displaying their merchandise. Illegal drugs in our country, such as marijuana, could be purchased in stores in Amsterdam. Obviously, theirs is a much more open and permissive culture than ours. Maybe that's why we saw so many young people in Amsterdam.

Amsterdam is a lovely city with canals, beautiful homes, and buildings. It's no wonder that the famous artists, "The Dutch Masters," were so successful. The views are breath-taking. For our last night's dinner in Amsterdam, Charlotte and I went across the street from our hotel and had a leisurely two-hour dinner, topped off with a fantastic apple, caramel, and whipped cream dessert. It was the best dessert that we had on the whole trip!

Brugge, Belgium

The next day found us traveling to Brugge, Belgium (brew-shh). It is a beautiful city with a river running through it, an old castle, and looks like it's right out of some medieval storybook. We bought a beautiful silk tapestry and a number of lace items and had them shipped home. That first night, we went to an enchanting violin concert in the castle.

The second day in Belgium began with a trip to a World War II Memorial and a museum dedicated to the allies for the fighting that took place near Bastogne. "The Battle of the Bulge" is another name given to that famous battle of WW II. The museum has thousands of items from both the Germans and the Allied Forces. There were light and heavy-duty weapons, jeeps, tanks, bazookas, uniforms, mess equipment, etcetera. There was also a large gift shop with hundreds of items for sale. We watched a film that incorporated U.S. Army news reels depicting actual coverage of some of the battles that had occurred in that area. Most of the film was biased coverage for the Americans, and I wondered to myself how contemporary Germans felt when they watched that same film.

Charlotte bought a book by Guy Franz Arend, entitled *Bastogne*. Arend was a Belgian who witnessed the battles in the area as a young man and later wrote many books about the battles in that part of the world. What seemed to me unique about Arend's book *Bastogne* was that he interviewed soldiers from both sides of the war after the war and included their comments, as well as their pictures and other related pictures to the battles. I had never read a book that had insights and perspectives from both sides of a battle.

On our last night in Belgium, Charlotte and I settled into our room and opened the windows for a magnificent view of the river. We had purchased locally freshly baked rolls, cheese, and wine that served as our dinner. Our stay in Belgium was too brief, and someday I would like to go back to Belgium.

Germany

We spent five days traveling across Germany, mainly on the Autobahn Highway while trying to avoid the big cities and their traffic. In preparation for our trip to the Czech Republic, we had spent our last night in Hoff, a German border town. What I remember most about Hoff was the Hotel Central near the German and Czech Republic border. The Hotel Central was a hotel with similar amenities to an American 4-Star Hotel. It was the most luxurious hotel that we stayed in during that entire trip.

On the eve of our first night, Mary Lou had decided that she wanted to go down to the hotel whirl pool and relax for awhile. She told us that she had slipped on a swimming suit and robe and had taken the elevator down to the whirl pool area. When she walked into the whirl pool area (she was explicit about this), she noticed that there were men lying on their backs under heat lamps in the area of the whirl pool. She was shocked to see that they were nude, and she quit looking at them after about ten minutes. Just kidding. She left immediately, and she told us later that registered nurses were not used to that kind of exposure. Right!

Czech Republic

We left our van in Hoff, Germany (An Amsterdam-related rental car agency) and we were met by our Czech Republic guide Janna (Yah-na) Bartosova. Janna is a beautiful and talented woman whom we had previously met through Charlie and Mary Lou Jirik. She had stayed with them when she had been on one of her recent trips to the United States. Part of our reason to travel to the Czech Republic was that Charlie Jirik wanted to see if he could find the home of his Czech grandfather, Frank Jirik.

When Janna knew that we would be coming to her country, she had volunteered to rent a van and be our guide for a few days. Charlie was one hundred percent Bohemian, and I, as a matter of fact am about two-thirds Norwegian and one-third Bohemian, if there is a viable way to distribute my heritage using a percent. Charlie could speak Bohemian in our part of the country, but the language has changed some in the Czech Republic. Janna was very helpful for Charlie and always tried to give him the current expression for the Bohemian/Czech language that he knew.

When we loaded our luggage into Janna's van, I was concerned about the reliability of the vehicle. In layman's terms, "It was a beater!" I have no idea how old the vehicle was, but I'd guess in the ten- to fifteen-year-old bracket. It was white and had a number of dents and the tires didn't look so hot. It was much smaller than the vehicle that we had rented. When she took off, she ground the gears in the transmission and had difficulty in getting the shift to cooperate in some of the gears. It was not a rental car, but one she had borrowed from a friend. I thought we might be lucky to go fifty miles in that van, let alone several hundred miles as would be needed to go to the places on our agenda. Crossing the border into the Czech Republic was a breeze as Janna smiled and made some cute remarks to the border patrol and froze them right in their tracks. She was an expert in manipulating men!

Karlovy Vary, Czech Republic

It was so obvious driving into the Czech Republic that it had been under communist control for so long. In our travels across Holland, Belgium, and Germany, the upkeep of the homes was pretty obvious. They were very neat and tidy with landscaping and many flowers. In the Czech Republic, the homes were plain gray concrete and there was little pride evidenced in their yards. I think it was mostly the lack of money and a culture that did not promote pride in ownership. On a previous trip, we had noticed the same differences between East and West Germany. Charlotte and I both loved the Czech crystal that we had purchased on a trip there in the early 1990s, and I wondered how much more we would buy our second time there.

Our first stop was in a city named Karlovy Vary. This was a city where the Russian communist dignitaries made frequent trips to bathe in the natural hot mineral waters, to party, and to let their wives shop for fine Bohemian Crystal. We had lunch at a corner café that didn't appear to be of the highest sanitary standards. That lunch would be my downfall later that evening.

Our first night in the Czech Republic was in a hotel of dubious distinction. There was an international economic conference going on at the same time in Prague and Janna said that was the reason that we had such mediocre hotel rooms. There were riots going on evolving around the international conference, and she was kept informed by one of her friends by cell phone so that we would have safe travel in the city. When the rest of the group went out to dinner that night, I stayed back in our room on a single bed with a fever and stomach flu. I figured the cause of the flu was the noontime lunch because I had had nothing to eat since lunch, other than bottled water that I had brought along from Germany earlier that day.

The second day in Prague, we toured the president's palace, Prague Castle, and Wencelas Square. We walked across the St. Charles Bridge, rode the street cars, and walked miles. We also shopped and purchased several pieces of Czech crystal. Janna warned us to avoid the men dressed in black fatigues. She said that they were associated with a criminal element in their society. We avoided them like the plague.

Lidice is a city approximately thirty miles northeast of Prague. During World War II, two members of a Czech resistance group thought by the Germans to be from Lidice lobbed a hand grenade into the open air vehicle of a German General Rhinehart Heydrich, the number two man in the German SS. The general was killed instantly. The German Army went to Lidice to seek revenge in the death of their general. They took boys whom they thought looked German and sent them to foster homes in Germany. They murdered all the rest of the boys and men in the village. Many of the women were raped and beaten. Jim Dalglish had relatives that had moved out of Lidice just before the outbreak of World War II. There is a huge memorial near where the massacre had occurred with statues representing mothers crying.

Cske Budejovice, Czech Republic

Cske Budejovice is the town where some of Charlie Jirik's relatives were baptized. We visited that church and were given a tour by a very nice priest. Janna continued to serve as our interpreter. We drove a few miles and arrived at a small village named Dralotesice. Janna stopped the van and asked a resident where we might find some records about Frank Jirik, Charlie's grandfather. The resident directed us down the road a few hundred feet where we saw some people standing outside a small building. Janna discovered that one of them was the mayor of the town; the mayor went inside the building and found the address where Frank Jirik had lived. We then drove just a couple of blocks and found the old homestead of Frank Jirik.

Frank Jirik's home was now owned by someone from Prague who used it as a summer retreat from the big city. The house was neat and clean and we took several pictures of Charlie and Mary Lou standing by the house before we left. Five out of the six members of our group had found something significant about their ancestors during our trip.

Our last little trip in the Czech Republic was to Janna's hometown, a couple of hours from Prague. When we arrived, we were treated first class by Janna's parents. Neither of them spoke English, but Janna made our visit very pleasant. Her father insisted that we have some liqueur that was pretty potent, and her mother had made a lovely lunch for us. They had a beautiful home and garden area. Janna's father was a building contractor; and with the fall of Communism, he had become a successful entrepreneur. Janna's parents were both hunters. They received a call while we were there from friends, who had shot a deer, but had lost the trail of the wounded deer. Their friends wanted Janna's parents help. Janna's mother was a beautiful and gracious woman and physically reminded me of Jackie Kennedy.

There were two times when Janna was driving the van that I thought we were headed for an accident. All of the roads, except near the major cities, are one lane each way. Janna had a real habit of "tailgating" trucks when we were on the highway. Two times she had pulled out to pass the trucks when another vehicle was coming right at us. Both times the trucks that we were passing and the on-coming vehicles both continued driving and swerved to the right, and we went between them!

When we left the Czech Republic, I'm certain that we had more merchandise in that vehicle then we could legitimately declare. When we stopped at the border checkpoint, Janna had gathered all of our passports and charmed the guards once again. They just smiled at her and waved us through.

Governor Jessie Ventura

Jessie Ventura was elected governor of Minnesota in November of 1998, by narrowly defeating the other two major party candidates: Hubert H. Humphrey III (Democrat) and Norman Coleman (Republican). None of them achieved thirty percent of the vote, but Jessie was still the victor.

Respect is very often just not given; it has to be earned. When we start a new job, move to a new neighborhood, or make new associations, we have to pay our "dues." In so many ways, our work or social cultures determine what is or is not acceptable behavior. Elected officials should be treated no better than the general public? Although, I know from personal experience that politicians are treated differently.

A couple of years ago, Governor Ventura was miffed that the governor's office was shown such little respect at the Republican National Convention. At that convention, the leader of the Minnesota Republican Delegation included in his announcement of delegate votes for Governor Bush, "…Minnesota Land of 10,000 lakes and one goofy governor…" A video tape of that announcement shown on Minnesota television news broadcasts showed many convention people enjoying the comment. I recall some years ago that similar remarks were also made about Governor Rudy Perpich, who, like Ventura, also had some idiosyncrasies.

Governor Ventura had a lot of national media exposure during his four years in office. Much of that attention was created by his surprise election. Ventura, however, contributed substantially more attention to himself through interviews in *Playboy Magazine*, comments he made on local as well as nationally televised shows, his books, refereeing professional wrestling, and the like. It was hard to take him very seriously. He seemed more concerned about making money through private ventures than his official duties. It was difficult to know when he was our Governor Ventura and when he was "winking-Jesse" on a nationally televised soap opera. People made fun of him in the media and on the streets. Many times I was embarrassed when some of his antics were brought up to me when I was attending a function outside the state of Minnesota.

He did have charisma. He did have a strong following; although if all of the people who said they had voted for him really had, he would have won the governor's race by a landslide. As his term as governor progressed, there were fewer and fewer people defending him. I noticed over time that he became a better speaker; and, in spite of his proclamations about the political process, he became a better politician. Under his watch the status of the state's coffers changed from a plus four billion to a negative four billion, in a little over four years.

Change is hard for a lot of us. We expect our governors to be more circumspect and politically smart. Ventura bragged a lot about once being a member of the combat group known as the Navy Seals. I believe rightfully so. However, the bulk of airtime on his weekly radio shows on Minneapolis radio station WCCO was spent boasting about one thing or another. Ventura was always battling with the media whom he often referred to as jackals. One of my mentors had once advised me, "Don't take on those who buy ink by the barrel." Ventura should have had such sage advice.

Governor Ventura's lack of higher education (I believe he only attended one semester at a community college) may have been a reason that he didn't support higher education in Minnesota very well. At one news conference, he was video taped telling students who were worried about financial aid reductions, "You figured out how to get to college now figure out how you can stay."

He treated the governor's office as a nine-to-five job where he was only needed from Monday to Friday.

I was glad when Jesse Ventura decided not to seek reelection as governor. I doubt if he would have been reelected anyway. I was surprised when the CNBC Television Network offered Ventura big bucks for a talk show, and I was not surprised to see that it only aired for a very short time. I have read recently that Ventura will lead a political seminar for undergraduate students at Harvard University. I am still baffled by his popularity.

May 1, 2001 in Glenville, MN

Glenville, Minnesota is a small town with a population of approximately 750 people. It is located near Interstate Highway 35 and about half way between Albert Lea, Minnesota to the north and Northwood, Iowa to the south, each of those communities is about six miles away traveling on ol' Highway 65. Albert Lea is by far the largest of the three communities with a population of approximately 18,000. All three communities are surrounded by farm land, rivers, creeks, and lakes. The primary small grain crops are corn and soy beans. The Glenville community is hardworking, honest, friendly, and close knit.

We moved to Glenville in 1998 as I had accepted the position of superintendent of schools for the newly merged Glenville-Emmons Independent School District 2886. The city of Emmons is located about a twenty-minute drive west of Glenville. I had been involved in two education mergers prior to this one, but all but one of my twenty years of administrative experience had been at the collegiate level. I did my best to make the merger transition as smooth as possible, and I'm proud of a number of accomplishments that we made over the two years that I served the district. I was not enjoying the superintendent's responsibilities nearly as much as the years I served as president in a technical college. Therefore, after thirty-five years in education, I decided in 2000 to take an early retirement. I had not imagined just how wonderful retirement could be. My wife had retired after over thirty years in education in 1999. We have been actively involved in our community since we arrived in 1998 and continue to be so at this writing.

In the spring of 2001 both Charlotte and I had been working on a number of volunteer projects in the Glenville community. On the evening of May 1, 2001, we were parked on Main Street in front of the Community Center. The community center is a brick building and is attached to the Glenville Volunteer Fire Department. There is a food preparation area, auditorium seating for approximately one hundred, and a couple of rest rooms. Monthly city council meetings are held there as well as a number of community organizations and gatherings. Charlotte and I were waiting in our car to attend a Glenville beautification project meeting, which was scheduled to begin at 7 p.m. There were a lot of people in the community that were interested in seeing what we could do to make Glenville a more attractive place to work, live, and play. We were at the wrong place. The meeting was at the Glenville American Legion, one block to the west.

At about 6:55 p.m. the rain turned to hail, so we decided to head for home to avoid having our automobile damaged by the hail. There were no severe weather sirens and we missed being in the direct path of the storm by a matter of seconds. In the time it took me to travel six blocks to our home, a tornado had struck Glenville quickly and caused several million dollars in property damage to homes, businesses, and public properties. Thankfully, there were no serious injuries as a result of the storm. The people who had gathered at the legion for the meeting crowded into the walk-in beer cooler for safety when the tornado hit. We live five blocks south of Main Street and I would estimate that the trip home took about one minute. As I pulled into the driveway the automatic garage door did not open, so I assumed that electrical lines were down.

I said to Charlotte, "Let's run for the basement this is bad."

She replied, "I want to put the car in the garage."

"Screw the car," I said.

"I'm not leaving the car outside."

"Okay, it's your life." I manually opened the garage door and I headed for the basement.

She joined me in the basement a couple minutes later and said she had put the car in the garage and closed the garage door. We had no power and it was dark in the basement so we lit up some candles and

I found a portable radio that didn't work.

After the storm had passed, we walked upstairs and outside. The sky was a grayish-green and there didn't seem to be any wind or rain. It was very calm and quiet except for the wailing sirens of emergency vehicles. There were small branches blown down lying around our yard. We walked around our property, and we could not see any major damage to trees nor to our house. We then proceeded to walk downtown and it was now only about 7:35 p.m.

As we approached downtown, we began to see more and more damage. The path of the tornado had gone approximately three blocks north and south of Main Street. Huge trees had fallen on homes, sometimes on vehicles, garages, or streets and caused considerable damage. We were shocked by the damage that had occurred to personal and public property in such a short period of time.

I am an amateur photographer, but I did not take pictures of the grief on people's faces, the property damage, or emergency people on the job that night. From a photographic standpoint, only I regret that I did not take pictures that night. The looks on people's faces were so sad that I could not take any pictures that night...it seemed to me that it would have been an invasion of their privacy. Furthermore, I chose not to take pictures of the many rescue personnel that came to our aid (sixteen fire departments, first aid personnel, sheriff's department, highway patrol, ambulances, civil defense, the National Guard, as well as our city government). I did, however, take several rolls of film the next day and have created photo scrapbooks and given them to the local fire department, the senior citizens center, and my banker friend Bob Krier.

I gave approximately two hundred pictures to a video company in Austin, Minnesota, who used still pictures, as well as amateur and professional video-taped materials, and made a composite video tape. We sold that video tape for beautification efforts as a result of the tornado.

Ted and Florence

My mother's humor has always been much more overt than my father's dry sense of humor. One time when I was riding in the back seat of their car (they had been married well over fifty years at the time), my mother looked at my dad, who was driving the car, and said, "How come we don't sit close together like we used to?"

My dad, continuing to drive, paused for awhile and dryly responded, "I haven't moved."

A Catholic Priest and Dan Rather

Several years ago, there was a visiting Catholic priest at St. Vincent de Paul Parish in Osseo, Minnesota, that did the following:

During his sermon the priest stopped and said, "Just suppose that Dan Rather, CBS News, or someone like him, was standing outside on the steps when you leave here today and he is going to beam live whatever your response is to his question. And let's suppose that his question will be, 'Why were you in this church today?' How will you respond to him?"

"Now, while you're thinking about your response for Dan Rather (who is not here today) I'm going to disconnect my microphone and bring a portable microphone with me so that I can beam your response to his question to the rest of the congregation. Remember his question will be, 'Why were you in this church today?'"

The priest disconnected his microphone and was given another by an alter boy and was walking down the steps to the congregation. My wife and I were in the third row from the front and I felt my mouth going dry and thoughts were racing through my mind, like, *Who does he think he is? I won't answer. What if I don't answer? What will my wife think? Who cares what she thinks. What will my kids think…what will my kids say? Why am I here today? Oh, he's almost down to the front pew and I'm sitting next to the aisle.*

There was absolute silence throughout the church, and I could see people around me looking at their feet so that they wouldn't have eye contact with the priest. When he reached the front row of pews, he stopped and lingered for what seemed like eternity. Then he turned around and went back up to the pulpit and said, "Did I make you think a little about why you are here today?"

There was an audible sigh of relief from the congregation. I thought about that a lot. I've grown since then and I try to know what I believe, and why I do what I do, most of the time anyway.

Printed in the United States
21803LVS00003BA/356